GLAD TIDINGS NEAR
Cumorah

GLAD TIDINGS NEAR
Cumorah

FIRSTHAND ACCOUNTS OF SACRED PLACES, ANGELIC VISITATIONS, AND ANCIENT RELICS

BY
BRUCE E. DANA

CFI
Springville, Utah

ISBN: 1-55517-723-9
e.1

Published by Cedar Fort Inc.
www.cedarfort.com

Distributed by:

Cover design by Nicole Cunningham
Cover design © 2004 by Lyle Mortimer

Printed in the United States of America
10 9 8 7 6 5 4 3 2 1

Printed on acid-free paper

Library of Congress Cataloging-in-Publication Data

Dana, Bruce E.
  Glad tidings near Cumorah / by Bruce E. Dana.
      p. cm.
  ISBN 1-55517-723-9 (pbk. : alk. paper)
  1. Book of Mormon.   I. Title.
  BX8627.D35 2003
  289.3'22--dc22

                    2003022168

ACKNOWLEDGMENTS

As I have written in my previous books, the reader is informed that without the support of my wife, Brenda, this work would never have been written. She truly has given me valuable time to research and write.

I am thankful for all of my children: Janalene, Connie, Michelle, Tami, Heather, Brooke, Benjamin, and Nathan, and for my parents, Edward and Shirley Dana, and my wife's parents, Max and Jody Lamb, for their constant love and devotion.

In writing this book, I am grateful to my publisher, Cedar Fort, Inc., for their confidence in publishing my previous four books. In particular, I am appreciative to my dear friend, Dennis "C" Davis, who has generously shared his vast knowledge of the gospel with me, and has reviewed my writings so that they will be doctrinally correct. There are other friends, my wife's parents, my mother, Jean Britt, and Ann Hunt who have taken the time to read all or a portion of my manuscript and given valuable comments and suggestions.

PREFACE

After long centuries of apostate darkness, the restoration of the gospel began on a beautiful spring day in 1820, in a place designated as the Sacred Grove. In this peaceful place, appropriately designated as a sacred garden, God the Father and his Son, Jesus Christ, physically appeared and verbally spoke to a young lad, Joseph Smith, Jr. This momentous visit commenced the Dispensation of the Fulness of Times. Glorious truths and doctrines were revealed in this place made sacred.

Besides this glorious appearance, an ancient Nephite prophet, Moroni, appeared to the boy-prophet and revealed many important truths of the gospel. This angelic visitant told him of a book that was deposited, written upon gold plates, giving an account of the ancient inhabitants of the American continent. Moroni also said that the fulness of the everlasting gospel was contained in it. Joseph Smith was also informed that specific instruments of revelation were deposited with the plates. After four years of visiting this sacred depository, Joseph was allowed to take the plates, and through the instruments of revelation, he was able to translate the *Book of Mormon*.

Though many of these teachings are not new to the Latter-day people, this book will present unique teachings and doctrines that are not widely known. With this introduction, let us begin our fascinating study of sacred places, angelic visitations, and instruments of revelation in the early history of The Church of Jesus Christ of Latter-day Saints.

TABLE OF CONTENTS

CHAPTER ONE
SACRED GARDENS

GARDEN OF EDEN

Since the creation of this earth, there have been many beautiful gardens. Whether it is large or small, a garden can be any cultivated plot of land that produces vegetables or fruits or herbs or flowers. Likewise, public recreation areas or parks are sometimes called botanical gardens. Besides these typical gardens, let us consider three that are classified as sacred.

When Adam and Eve were born on this earth,[1] they lived in a beautiful and pristine place called the Garden of Eden, which was paradisiacal in nature.[2] Though we do not know the exact size of Eden, we may properly believe that its boundaries were confined to several acres in a vast land area. As Elder Joseph Fielding Smith has explained, "We are committed to the fact that Adam dwelt on this American Continent. But when Adam dwelt here, it was not the American Continent, nor was it the Western Hemisphere, for all of the land was in one place, and all the water was in one place. There was no Atlantic Ocean separating the hemispheres."[3]

The following is taken from an article that was printed in the *Juvenile Instructor*: "From the Lord, Joseph learned that Adam had dwelt on the land of America, and that the Garden of Eden was located where Jackson County, Missouri now is."[4] To give further explanation about the exact location of this Garden, we find that the Temple Block in Jackson County stands on the identical spot where once stood the Garden of Eden.[5] Therefore, this glorious garden was located on the American Continent "where the City Zion, or the New Jerusalem, will be built," and on August 2, 1831 the Prophet Joseph Smith dedicated the site for the temple on a spot a short distance west of the court house in Independence, Missouri.[6]

According to the Prophet Joseph Smith, when Adam and Eve transgressed, they were expelled from the Garden of Eden and traveled in a northerly direction some 85 miles to settle in a place that has been revealed as Adam-ondi-Ahman. Elder Bruce R. McConkie provides this information: "Apparently the area included was a large one; at least, the revelations speak of the *land*, the *valley*, and the *mountains* of Adam-ondi-Ahman.[7] They tell us that Christ himself 'established the foundations of Adam-ondi-Ahman' (D&C 78:15-16), and that it included the place known as Spring Hill, Daviess County, Missouri (D&C 116)" (Italics in quote).

"Far West, Missouri, also appears to be included in the land of Adam-ondi-Ahman. On April 17, 1838, the Lord commanded his saints to be assembled at Far West, which place, he said, was holy ground; and there they were to build a city.' (D&C 115)

Elder McConkie then explains the significance of this sacred place:

"On May 19, 1838, Joseph Smith and a number of his associates stood on the remainder of the pile of stones at a place called Spring Hill, Daviess County, Missouri. There the Prophet taught them that Adam again would visit in the Valley of Adam-ondi-Ahman, holding a great council as a prelude to the great and dreadful day of the

Lord (*Meditation and Atonement*, pp. 69-70) at this council, all who have held keys of authority will give an accounting of their stewardship to Adam. Christ will then come, receive back the keys, and thus take one of the final steps preparatory to reigning personally upon the earth (Dan. 7:9-14; *Teachings*, p. 157)."[8]

At the Second Coming of our Lord, "the earth will receive its paradisiacal glory," which means it will return again to conditions similar as they were in the Garden of Eden, prior to the fall (Isaiah 51:3; Ezek. 36:35).

GARDEN OF GETHSEMANE

Following significant events that transpired at the last Passover meal eaten by our Lord in Jerusalem, John tell us that Jesus "went forth with his disciples over the brook Cedron, *where was a garden*, into the which he entered, and his disciples" (John 18:1-2) (Italics added).

Concerning this special garden, Elder James E. Talmage has written this description: "Jesus and his eleven apostles went forth from the house in which they had eaten, passed through the city gate, which was usually left open at night during a public festival, crossed the ravine of Cedron, or more accurately Kidron, brook, and entered an olive orchard known as Gethsemane, on the slope of Mount Olivet."[9]

Then, in an endnote, he provides this informative explanation: "The name [Gethsemane] means 'oil-press' and probably has reference to a mill maintained at the place for the extraction of oil from olives there culti-vated. John refers to the spot as a garden, from which designation we may regard it as an enclosed space of private ownership . . . ."[10]

We cannot with surety reconstruct the events that transpired in the Garden of Gethsemane that evening. From what has been written by the gospel writers, we may safely believe that our Lord—in company with Peter, James, and John—spent several agonizing hours in this olive orchard.

In addition to various prayers offered by our Lord to his Father, we learn from Luke that "there appeared an angel unto him from heaven, strengthening him" (Luke 22:43). Regarding this angel, Elder McConkie has written these thought-provoking words: "The angelic ministrant is not named . . . and if we might indulge in speculation, we would suggest that the angel who came into this second Eden [which is the Garden of Gethsemane] was the same person who dwelt in the first Eden [which is the Garden of Eden]. At least Adam, who is Michael, the archangel—the head of the whole heavenly hierarchy of angelic ministrants—seems the logical one to give aid and comfort to his Lord on such a solemn occasion. Adam fell, and Christ redeemed men from the fall; theirs was a joint enterprise, both parts of which were essential for the salvation of the Father's children."[11]

From the Joseph Smith Translation of Luke, we read: "And being in an agony, he prayed more earnestly; and he sweat as it were great drops of blood falling down to the ground." Regarding our Lord's redemptive suffering, we use the words written in the *Book of Mormon*, as revealed by an angel to King Benjamin: "And lo, he shall suffer temptations, and pain of body . . . even more than man can suffer, except it be unto death; for behold, blood cometh from every pore, so great shall be his anguish from the wickedness and the abominations of his people" (See Mosiah 3:7).

Thus, in this special garden our beloved Lord took upon himself the burden of the sins of the world; accordingly, based upon the condition of repentance, mankind would be redeemed from the fall. This quiet, sacred place is to be remembered with reverence as the garden where our Savior performed a redemptive sacrifice that was only reserved for a God.

SACRED GROVE

It is important to understand that the Dispensation of the Fulness of Times was to commence in the year 1820 and everything connected with this glorious event had to be in place. Joseph Smith, Jr. must be living in a home near Palmyra, New York. The Smith family must be religious, as well as lovingly supportive of each member of that household. An unusual excitement on the subject of religion must be in motion in that region. Young Joseph must read a passage from James in the *Bible*, which would arouse a great desire in him to ask of God for an answer. Likewise, a grove of trees must be close to the Smith home so that God the Father and His Son could appear in privacy to the great Seer of the latter-days. Truly, omnipotent wisdom had left nothing to chance in these matters. The hand of the Lord had planned and prepared all of those things in advance.

Paraphrasing the words of Elder Joseph Fielding Smith, we find that following three years of crop failures and a year of lingering illness for various members, the Joseph Smith, Sr. family made a decision to move from Vermont to western New York, where they heard it was a milder climate and a more fertile region. During a family counsel, it was decided to purchase about one hundred acres of land, located about two miles south of Palmyra on the border of Manchester. In the year 1815, western New York was sparsely settled and land was inexpensive to purchase. At the time of their arrival in Palmyra, two of the older boys, Alvin and Hyrum, were able to assist in making a new home. With their father they began clearing the newly acquired land from a dense growth of trees. Besides this challenging task, they did a day's labor for other people, as opportunity afforded, to obtain needed money to meet their financial obligations. During that first year, by hard work, these three cleared about thirty acres of timber and were able to pay most of their first payment on this land that was not yet ready for farming.

About four years after the arrival of the Smith family in Palmyra, they moved to the farm where they built a four-room home that was later increased by the addition of sleeping rooms on the rear. It was while living in this residence that Joseph Smith, Jr. received various visions.[12]

EVENTS THAT LED TO THE FIRST VISION

With sincerity, Joseph Smith, Jr. related events that led to the First Prayer and Vision in a sacred grove of trees that has been designated as a *garden*. A small portion of his comments are presented:

"Some time in the second year after our removal to Manchester, there was in the place where we lived an unusual excitement on the subject of religion . . . Indeed, the whole district of country seemed affected by it, and great multitudes united themselves to the different religious parties, which created no small stir and division amongst the people . . .

"In the midst of this war of words and tumult of opinions, I often said to myself, what is to be done? Who of all these parties are right; or are they all wrong together? If any one of them be right, which is it, and how shall I know it? While I was thus laboring under the extreme difficulties caused by the contests of these parties of religionists, I was one day reading in the Epistle of James, first chapter and fifth verse, which reads:

'If any of you lack wisdom, let him ask of God, that giveth to all men liberally, and upbraideth not; and it shall be given him.'

"Never did any passage of scripture come with more power to the heart of man than this did at this time to mine . . . I reflected on it again and again, knowing that if any person needed wisdom from God, I did . . . At length I came to the conclusion that I must either remain in darkness and confusion, or else I must do as James directs, that is, ask of God . . . So, in accordance with this, my determination to ask of God, I retired to the woods to make the attempt. It was on the morning of a beautiful, clear day, early in the spring of eighteen hundred and twenty. It was the first time in my life that I had made such an attempt, for amidst all my anxieties I had never as yet made the attempt to pray vocally"[13] (Italics added).

THE WOODS—A SACRED GARDEN

Concerning the woods where Joseph Smith, Jr. went to "ask of God," we find that "directly west of the Smith home, a few hundred yards distant, yet on their own farm, was a beautiful grove sufficiently dense and removed from the road to give the necessary seclusion the youth desired."[14] It is believed that this particular grove of trees was about 400 years old when the Smith family moved to the site around 1818.[15] As has been mentioned, during the first year the Smith family cleared about thirty acres of trees that reached the heights of up to 125 feet and diameters of 6 feet or more. The next year or so, they cleared another thirty acres of heavy timber and converted it into a tillable farm. In addition to this cleared land that was used for farming and gardening, we learn that the Sacred Grove was part of a fifteen-acre wooded area at the farm's west end where the Smith family had a sugar orchard of from twelve to fifteen hundred maple trees, which were tapped from making maple syrup or sugar.[16] Therefore, by divine providence this special 15-acre forest was specifically prepared centuries early by the Father and the Son so that they could appear to Joseph in sacred seclusion on a beautiful spring day in 1820.

At the April 1906 General Conference of the Church, Elder George Albert Smith related a special trip made to Palmyra, New York. Said he:

"I believe it may be interesting to this great congregation if I shall detail to you some of the circumstances with the recent visit made by President [Joseph F.] Smith, and a number of members of the Church, to the state of Vermont, where a beautiful monument was dedicated to the memory of the Prophet Joseph Smith.

"On the 18th day of December last there left this city, in a private [railroad] car, 30 souls, 29 of whom had been invited by President Smith to accompany him to the dedication of the monument. I desire to say that we all, including President Smith, paid our own expenses . . . ."

Later in his talk, he revealed the following information:

"We boarded the train on Christmas night and were taken westward. On the morning of the 26th, we arrived at the little station of Palmyra. There we found carriages awaiting us, and we began a tour of that section of the country, visiting places of much interest to the Latter-day Saints. We went to the former home of the father of the Prophet Joseph Smith, where Joseph came with the plates after he had received them from the hand of Moroni, and where, it is said, he received the manifestations of the angel, who appeared to him three times in one night. We went into the grove where Joseph had knelt down and asked the Lord to inform him which church he should join. We were impressed to sing, in that hallowed place, the beautiful Mormon Sunday school hymn: 'Joseph Smith's First Prayer.' Mr. [William Avery] Chapman, who owns the property and who accorded us ever possible courtesy, informed us that the grove we went into had never had a tree cut down. The property had fallen into the hands of his father after our people had moved away and he had held these woods sacred, and they took their timber from other groves around there . . . ."[17]

Likewise, owners of the farm previous to Mr. Chapman maintained and preserved the grove, associating it with Joseph Smith's vision. It is worth noting that in 1907 the Church purchased the farm and grove from Mr. Chapman and these sites have formed the center of the Church historical sites program.[18]

In a Conference Report of 1949, Elder Thomas E. McKay, who is the brother of President David O. McKay, spoke of the power of prayer: "We are here today, brethren and sisters, because this great Church of ours has been organized—a wonderful organization—established for the last time, never to be taken away from the earth or given to another people, and all in answer to a prayer, *a prayer in a garden, the Sacred Grove* . . . "[19] (Italics added).

Appropriately, the Sacred Grove has been described as a garden. Therefore, we know of three sacred gardens: The Garden of Eden, where Adam and Eve once lived; the Garden of Gethsemane, where our Savior atoned for our sins, based upon repentance; and the Garden of the Sacred Grove, where the Father and Son appeared to Joseph Smith, Jr., in 1820 and ushered in the Dispensation of the Fulness of Times.

CHAPTER TWO
JOSEPH SMITH WAS FOREORDAINED

The Latter-day Saint people firmly believe that the Lord's chosen servants are foreordained to serve in their various callings. To Jeremiah of the Old Testament, the Lord said: "Before I formed thee in the belly I knew thee; and before thou camest forth out of the womb I sanctified thee, and I ordained thee a prophet unto the nations" (Jeremiah 1:5).

In the Book of Mormon, we are informed that nearly six hundred years before their mortal birth, Nephi saw in vision the Lamb of God, the Twelve Apostles, and the Virgin of Nazareth, who would become the mortal mother of Jesus Christ (1 Nephi 11: 12)

Abraham, another Old Testament prophet, was privileged to see one of the grandest visions ever given to mortal man. In it he saw "the intelligences that were organized before the world was; and among all these there were many of the noble and great ones," he said. "And God saw these souls that they were good, and he stood in the midst of them, and he said: These I will make my rulers; for he stood among those that were spirits, and he saw that they were good." Accordingly, these noble and great ones included all of the prophets and apostles and leaders of all ages who would serve in the Lord's kingdom on earth. Then, the Lord directed his remarks to this great man and declared: "Abraham, thou art one of them; thou wast chosen before thou wast born" (Abraham 3:22-23).

"Indeed," says Elder Bruce R. McConkie, "all of the prophets of all the ages; all of the Lord's witnesses who have held apostolic power; all of the holy and righteous men who have been commissioned to carry the message of salvation to the world; all who have been appointed to minister for the spiritual needs of the sons of men—all were foreordained."[20]

Continuing with his words, Elder McConkie has appropriately written: "As it was with Abraham, so it was with Joseph Smith. Each was foreordained to preside over a great gospel dispensation . . . There have been many prophets, and numerous apostles, but there have been few heads of dispensations . . . Thus, Joseph Smith ranks with the dozen or score of the mightiest spiritual giants who have so far dwelt upon the earth."[21]

Concerning callings to serve in the Lord's ministry on earth, we read what the Prophet himself revealed: "Every man who has a calling to minister to the inhabitants of the world was ordained to that very purpose in the Grand Council of heaven before this world was. [He then adds this choice comment:] I suppose I was ordained to this very office in that Grand Council."[22]

Not only did Joseph become the first apostle and prophet in modern times, but he also became the head of the final dispensation. All of this transpired because of his foreordination in the premortal existence.

"IF ANY OF YOU LACK WISDOM"

Joseph Smith, Jr. was born December 23, 1805, at Sharon, Windsor County, Vermont. Having moved with his family near Palmyra, New York, he states that in the spring of 1820, "I was at this time in my fifteenth year"

(Joseph Smith—History 1:7). Meaning, he was approaching his fifteenth birthday in December. "Some time in the second year after our removal to Manchester, there was in the place where we lived an unusual excitement on the subject of religion . . .

"During this time of great excitement my mind was called up to serious reflection and great uneasiness; but though my feelings were deep and often poignant, still I keep myself aloof from all these parties, though I attended their several meetings as often as occasion would permit . . .

"My mind at times was greatly excited, the cry and tumult were so great and incessant . . .

"In the midst of this war of words and tumult of opinions, I often said to myself: What is to be done? Who of all these parties are right; or, are they all wrong together? If any one of them be right, which is it, and how shall I know it?" (Joseph Smith—History 1:8-10)

Because of his valiancy in the premortal life, Joseph brought with him all of the talents and spiritual ability he had abundantly acquired through long ages of obedience and progression in this realm. Being spiritually attuned, he "was one day reading the Epistle of James, first chapter and fifth verse, which reads: *'If any of you lack wisdom, let him ask of God, that giveth to all men liberally, and upbraideth not; and it shall be given him'*" (Joseph Smith History—1:11) (Italics added).

Though these words have a universal application to all who are seeking to know the word of God, we discover, as Elder McConkie has powerfully written, ". . . yet they were preserved through the ages for the especial guidance of that prophet who should usher in the dispensation of the fulness of times."[23]

At various times and places, people are prompted to do something. If those individuals are sensitive to these impressions, they will be blessed. Direction and answers will come by different means. For as Elder Boyd K. Packer has explained: "Some answers will come from reading the scriptures, some from hearing speakers. And, occasionally, when it is important, some will come by very direct and powerful inspiration. The promptings will be clear and unmistakable."[24]

Young Joseph was perplexed and desired to know which church was right, or if they were all wrong, and how he would know it. After reading this special scripture in James, he says: *"Never did any passage of scripture come with more power to the heart of man than this did at this time to mine"* (Joseph Smith–History 1:12) (Italics added).

The time had come for the ushering in of the last and great gospel dispensation. This boy-prophet was the noble and great one who had been prepared from all eternity to receive the inspired word and act accordingly.

"The Spirit of God rested mightily upon him," says Elder McConkie. "Not even Enoch and Abraham and Moses and the ancient prophets had been overpowered by such yearnings for truth and salvation as then filled Joseph's soul . . . ."[25]

The Prophet says that this impression "seemed to enter with great force into every feeling of my heart." As Elder Packer has explained, this was a "very direct and powerful inspiration."

Notwithstanding what happened, it is important to point out that Joseph did not immediately go and ask God for an answer. He says, *"I reflected on it again and again,* knowing that if any person needed wisdom from

God, I did . . . *At length* I came to the *conclusion* that I must either remain in darkness and confusion, or else I must do as James directs, that is, ask of God" (Joseph Smith—History 1:12-13) (Italics added).

Then, after he *concluded* that he must ask of God, he says, "I . . . came to the *determination* to 'ask of God'" (Joseph Smith—History 1:13) (Italics added). Though we are not informed of how long this process took, we may safely assume that it involved several days of serious pondering. It is equally important to know that the Lord allows every person his or her agency to act upon an impression. Likewise, as Elder Packer has truthfully written, "It is good to learn when you are young that spiritual things cannot be forced."[26]

Though the time was appointed for the ushering in of the final dispensation, and Joseph was foreordained to be the head of this dispensation, the Lord allowed this young lad his agency to act upon this powerful inspiration. Joseph had to make the determination that he would ask God for an answer to his questions. The Lord could not, nor would he, force Joseph Smith, Jr. to make that determination. Accordingly, agency is one of the greatest gifts that God gives to every individual who is born on this earth.

A BEAUTIFUL SPRING DAY

After seriously pondering upon this special scripture found in James, young Joseph says that "in accordance with this, my determination to ask of God, I retired to the woods to make the attempt. It was on the morning of a beautiful, clear day, early in the spring of eighteen hundred and twenty" (Joseph Smith—History 1:14).

Many Latter-day Saints have wondered what day Joseph went into the grove of trees to seek an answer from God. For some reason, the Prophet never revealed this information.

On April 6, 1930, President Charles W. Nibley, Second Counselor in the First Presidency, spoke of the First Vision. Said he:

"The Prophet Joseph recites in his own story that it was early in the spring of 1820, one hundred and ten years ago, when he went into the woods to pray. I like to think of that . . . as being on the sixth day of April. We have no revelation for it—that the Prophet Joseph Smith received his first manifestation on the *sixth day of April.* It was the greatest vision ever given to mortal man; for both the Father and the Son plainly manifested themselves before his eyes and spoke to him. I believe that that was on the sixth day of April . . ."[27] (Italics added).

In a published book, *Three Timely Treasures*, Leon M. Strong has expressed a similar opinion. He writes:

"The last and final dispensation is now with us, being ushered in by the Prophet Joseph Smith in the sacred grove *probably on April 6, 1820.*" Then, in a footnote, he provides this information: "[Elder] Orson F. Whitney, in June of 1931, told the present writer that even though there is no written record extant [to be in existence] saying that the Prophet's vision of the Father and the Son took place on April 6, it is nevertheless *good tradition* in the Church. Charles W. Nibley of the First Presidency apparently thought this was the correct date. See Comprehensive History of the Church 6:543"[28] (Italics added).

Whether or not this "beautiful, clear day, early in the spring" was April 6, 1820, it is important to emphasize that April 6 has significant meaning to the Latter-day Saint people. The following information will illustrate this significance:

As to when our Savior was born to his mortal mother, Mary, there are a number of unanswered questions surrounding his birth. One of these is the month, day, and year that this blessed event transpired. There are a variety of scholarly opinions, both in and out of the Church, on this subject. In a book that is approved by the Church, *Jesus the Christ*, Elder James E. Talmage has written these informative words: "We believe that Jesus Christ was born in Bethlehem of Judea, April 6, B.C. 1" (p. 104).

Gordon B. Hinckley, who was then a member of the Council of Twelve Apostles, President Spencer W. Kimball, and President Harold B. Lee all state that it was the sixth of April that Jesus Christ was born.[29]

Regarding the month, day, and year when Jesus died, Elder Orson Pratt says: "We have already brought the testimony of chronologists to prove that he was crucified on Friday, the 6th of April" (As written in Millennial Star, 28:810, dated December 22, 1866). Then, in an address delivered in the Tabernacle, in Salt Lake City, Utah, on April 10, 1870, he said: "We find [from the *Book of Mormon*] that the ancient Israelites on this continent had a sign given of the exact time of the crucifixion and a revelation of the exact time of the Savior's birth, and according to their reckoning, they made him thirty-three years and a little over three days old from the time of his birth to the time that he hung upon the cross" (As recorded in *Journal of Discourses*, Volume 13, pages 126-127).

Lastly, from the Prophet Joseph Smith himself in

1833: "On the 6th of April . . . it being just 1800 years since the Savior laid down his life . . . " (*Documentary History of the Church*, 1:336-337).

The Church of Jesus Christ of Latter-day Saints was formerly organized on the sixth day of April, 1830, at Fayette, New York, in the home of Peter Whitmer, Sr. At the formal organization, six members were present: Joseph Smith, Oliver Cowdery, Hyrum Smith, Peter Whitmer, Jr., David Whitmer and Samuel H. Smith. Previous to this day, each of these men had been baptized. They were again baptized on that memorable day, April 6, 1830.[30]

Every April and October a General Conference of the Church is held in Salt Lake City, Utah. These conference sessions are held on a Saturday and a Sunday. At the April Conference, one of these two-day sessions is either April 6th or as close to that day as possible.

Based upon what has been presented, the reader must decide whether or not that "beautiful, clear day, early in the spring of eighteen hundred and twenty" was April 6, 1820. Someday, in the providence of the Lord, we trust that this information will be revealed.

Returning again to the Prophet's words, he says that "in accordance with this, my *determination* to ask of God, I retired to the woods to make the attempt. . . . It was the first time in my life that I had made such an attempt, for amidst all my anxieties *I had never as yet made the attempt to pray vocally*" (Joseph Smith—History 1:14) (Italics added). Evidently, this young man had always expressed his private prayers silently. Because they were religious, we may properly assume that the Smith family said a blessing on their food, and each, in turn, gave a vocal thanks to God for their meal.

When Joseph entered the woods to pray that beautiful spring day, it was the time when foreordination and agency came together. Joseph finally made the determination to vocally pray and ask of God important questions.

"To carry forward his own purposes among men and nations," says Elder McConkie, "the Lord *foreordained* chosen spirit children in pre-existence and assigned them to come to earth at particular times and places so that they might aid in furthering the divine will. These pre-existence appointments, made 'according to the foreknowledge of God the Father' (1 Pet. 1:2), simply designated certain individuals to perform missions which the Lord in his wisdom knew they had the talents and capacities to do"[31] (Italics in quotation).

Joseph Smith, Jr. was foreordained to become the head of this the final dispensation because the Lord in his wisdom knew he had the talent and capacity to accomplish that important mission. What transpired next in the grove of trees has no equal in history.

CHAPTER THREE
VARIOUS ACCOUNTS
OF THE FIRST VISION

The foundation of The Church of Jesus Christ of Latter-day Saints is the story of the First Vision. Of all the mysteries of the gospel, this one has caused countless numbers of people to either decry it or testify of its truthfulness. Accordingly, it is the greatest truth or the greatest fraud. As such, we continue with the Prophet's narrative: "After I had retired to the place where I had previously designed to go, having looked around me, I kneeled down and began to offer up the desires of my heart to God" (Joseph Smith—History 1:15).

As has been previously written, a grove of trees must be close to the Smith home so that God the Father and his Son could appear in privacy to the great Seer of the latter-days. With agency in full force, we may properly believe that being spiritually attuned, Joseph was inspired to select the woods near his family home to ask of God. Accordingly, the grove of trees nearby became the "place where [he] had previously designed to go."

While in the woods, it is worth noting that Joseph "looked around" to see if he was alone. Whether this looking was a natural reaction, or he sensed that some unseen person was watching him, we are not informed. Having satisfied himself that he was alone, he "kneeled down and began to offer up the desires of [his] heart to God." This young lad says, "I had scarcely done so, when immediately I was seized upon by some power which overcame me, and had such and astonishing influence over me as to bind my tongue so that I could not speak. Thick darkness gathered around me, and it seemed to me for a time as if I were doomed to sudden destruction" (Joseph Smith—History 1:15).

This statement is from the official version of the First Vision. In addition to this version, there are other accounts that have been printed. Four were researched and published by BYU [Brigham Young University] Studies in the spring of 1969, on pages 280, 284, 290, and 296. Another version was printed in the *New York Spectator*, September 23, 1843. This account was written in *Dialogue: A Journal of Mormon Thought*, in autumn of 1966, page 43. Each account contains slight variations from the official version, but nothing that has or will cast doubt on the truthfulness of this transcendent event. The reader is to be reminded that Joseph Smith, Jr. was constantly hated and persecuted for relating this vision. From the official version, we read his explanatory words:

"I soon found, however, that *my telling the story* had excited a great deal of prejudice against me among professors of religion, and was the cause *of great persecution*, which continued to increase; and though I was an obscure boy, only between fourteen and fifteen years of age, and my circumstances in life such as to make a boy of no consequences in the world, yet men of high standing would take notice sufficient to excite the public mind against me, and create a bitter persecution; and this was common among all the sects—all united to persecute me" (Joseph Smith—History 1:22) (Italics added).

Because of this reaction, whenever the Prophet

related the First Vision, he was careful how he presented this sacred event and adapted it to the audience he was telling. Accordingly, various versions arose in order not to incur undue persecution. Besides sharing in this chapter what is written in the official version, portions of the various accounts will be presented for comparison. The reader is informed that the Brigham Young University Studies will be referred to as the BYU version. Other accounts will be self-identifying.

"I HEARD A NOISE BEHIND ME"

On page 284 of the BYU version, Joseph says that he "called on the Lord for the first time in the place above stated, or in other words, I made a fruitless attempt to pray. My tongue seemed to be swollen in my mouth, so that I could not utter, *I heard a noise behind me like some one walking towards me.*" Though he audibly heard this sound, he says, "I strove again to pray, but could not; *the noise of walking seemed to draw nearer.*" Whether he was alarmed, or naturally curious, or both, he states, "I sprang upon my feet and looked around, *but saw no person, or thing that was calculated to produce the noise of walking*" (Italics added).

Satan is a spirit personage who does not have a tangible body of flesh and bones; yet, by Joseph being spiritually attuned, he was able to hear Lucifer physically walking toward him. Very few prophets have seen Satan, let alone have heard him walking. From this account, we can more fully understand, even at age fourteen, how spiritually gifted Joseph was.

Returning to the official version, it reads: "But exerting all my powers to call upon God to deliver me out of the power of this enemy which had seized upon me, and at the very moment when I was ready to sink into despair and abandoned myself to destruction—not to an imaginary ruin, but to the power of some actual being from the unseen world, who had such marvelous power as I had never before felt in any being . . . " (Joseph Smith—History 1:16).

In a published book, Elder George Q. Cannon wrote the following description: "It was one morning early in springtime of the year 1820 that Joseph felt the earnest promptings and adopted the holy resolve. He walked into the depths of a wood, which stood near his home, *and sought a little glade* [an open space surrounded by woods]. There, in trembling humility, but with faith which thrilled his soul—alone, unseen of man, he fell upon his knees and lifted his voice in prayer to God. While he was calling upon the almighty, *a subtle and malignant power seized him and stilled his utterance.* Deep darkness enveloped him; *he felt he was in the grasp of Satan, and that the destroyer was exerting all the power of hell to drag him to sudden destruction*"[32] (Italics added).

Elder Cannon was ordained an apostle, at age 33 on August 26, 1860, by President Brigham Young. Though we are not specifically informed, we may safely assume that some of the information written by Elder Cannon came from President Young, who heard the Prophet Joseph Smith relate experiences associated with the First Vision that were not printed in the official version.

In support of what Elder Cannon wrote about the glade, or open space, the *New York Spectator* version reads: "I immediately went out into the woods where my father *had a clearing*, and I kneeled down, and prayed, saying, 'O Lord, what church shall I join?'" (Italics added).

However, on page 296 of the BYU version, the Prophet does not say that he went to a glade, or a clearing in the grove, but that he *"retired to a secret place* in a grove and began to call upon the Lord" (Italics added). Being young and inquisitive, Joseph would have naturally spent several hours, over the course of time, exploring and playing in the woods near his home. Therefore, he knew of several places that he could play and hide and not be seen. In this 15-acre wooded area, more than likely there were *various, small open spaces* that had been *cleared*, and were considered *secret places* to young Joseph.

"I SAW A PILLAR OF LIGHT"

Returning again to the official version, the Prophet says, ". . . just at this moment of great alarm, *I saw a pillar of light exactly over my head, above the brightness of the sun*, which descended gradually until it fell upon me.

"It no sooner appeared than I found myself delivered from the enemy which held me bound. When the light rested upon me I saw two Personages, whose brightness and glory defy all description, standing above me in the air . . . " (Joseph Smith—History 1:16-17) (Italics added).

Likewise, on page 280 of the BYU version, it reads: ". . . the Lord heard my cry in the wilderness and while in the attitude of calling upon the Lord in the 16th [Note: not his 15th year] year of my age *a pillar of light above the brightness of the sun at noon day come down from above and rested upon me* and I was filled with the spirit of God . . . " (Italics added).

The official version is identical to the BYU version, as written on page 290. It reads: "I saw a pillar of light exactly over my head, above the brightness of the sun, which descended gradually until it fell upon me . . . ."

Quoting from another BYU version, on page 296, *The Wentworth Letter*, Joseph says that the personages were "*surrounded with a brilliant light which eclipsed the sun at noon-day*" (Italics added).

In the *New York Spectator* version, Joseph simply says, "Directly I *saw a light* . . . " (Italics added).

Interestingly, on page 284 of the BYU version, The Prophet explains: "*A pillar of fire appeared above my head*; which presently rested down upon me, and filled me with unspeakable joy" (Italics added).

This BYU version is supported by what Elder Orson Pratt said in a sermon that was delivered in the Tabernacle, at Salt Lake City, Utah, February 24, 1869, as printed in the *Journal of Discourses*. Said he:

"The heavens, as it were, were opened to him, or in other words, a glorious pillar of light like the brightness of the sun appeared in the heavens above him, and approached the spot where he was praying; his eyes were fixed upon it and his heart was lifted up in prayer before the Most High. He saw the light gradually approaching him until it rested upon the tops of the trees. *He beheld that the leaves upon the trees were not consumed by it*, although its brightness, apparently, was sufficient, as he at first thought, *to consume everything before it*. But the trees were not consumed by it, and it continued to descend until it rested upon him and enveloped him in its glorious rays. When he was thus *encircled about this pillar of fire*, his mind was caught away from every object that surrounded him, and he was filled with the visions of the almighty, and he saw, *in the midst of this glorious pillar of fire,* two glorious personages, whose *countenances shone with an exceeding great luster . . ."*[33] (Italics added).

Five years later at the new Tabernacle, Elder Pratt again spoke on this subject. Said he:

"While thus praying, with all his heart, he discovered in the heavens above him, *a very bright and glorious light,* which gradually descended towards the earth, and when it reached the tops of the trees which overshadowed him, *the brightness was so great that he expected to see the leaves of the tree consumed by it . . .*

"Mr. Smith had this vision before he was fifteen years old . . . "[34] (Italics added).

Though there are differences in these accounts, they provide supplemental information to the official version. We are most grateful that these various accounts have been published concerning this great appearance by the Father and the Son to Joseph Smith, Jr.

"I SAW TWO PERSONAGES"

From the official version, the Prophet says, "I saw a pillar of light exactly over my head, above the brightness of the sun, which descended gradually until it fell upon me.

"It no sooner appeared than I found myself delivered from the enemy which held me bound. When the light rested upon me in the air *I saw two Personages,* whose brightness and glory defy all description, standing above me in the air. One of them spake unto me, calling me by name and said, pointing to the other—*This is my Beloved Son. Hear Him!"* (Joseph Smith—History 1:17) (Italics added).

To more fully understand the significance of this vision, we turn to the writings of Elder George Q. Cannon:

" . . . the deep gloom was rolled away and he saw a brilliant light. A pillar of celestial fire, far more glorious than the brightness of the noon-day sun, appeared directly above him. The defeated power fled with the darkness; and Joseph's spirit was free to worship and marvel at his deliverance. Gradually the light descended until it rested upon him; and he saw, standing above him in the air, enveloped in the pure radiance of the fiery pillar, two personages of incomparable beauty, alike in form and feature, and clad alike in snowy raiment. Sublime, dazzling, they filled his soul with awe. At length, One, calling Joseph by name, stretched His shining arm towards the Other, and said: 'THIS IS MY BELOVED SON: HEAR HIM!'"[35]

On page 280 of the BYU version, it reads: "I saw the Lord and he spake unto me saying Joseph my son thy sins are forgiven thee, go thy way, walk in my statures and keep my commandments . . ."

This account in no way disputes what the official version says. God the Father told Joseph that Jesus was his beloved Son and that he should hear him. In this version, we are fortunate to read a portion of what our Lord told the boy-prophet.

From the BYU version, on page 284, we notice a slight variation. Joseph says: "*A personage appeared* in the midst of this pillar of flame, which was spread all around and yet nothing consumed." Then, he explains: "*Another personage* soon appeared like unto the first; he said unto me thy sins are forgiven thee. He testified also unto me that Jesus Christ is the son of God."

27

In support of this account, the *New York Spectator* version reads: "Directly I saw a light, and then a glorious personage in the light, and then another personage, and the first person said to the second, 'Behold my Beloved Son, hear him.' I then addressed this second person, saying, 'O Lord, what church shall I join?' He replied, 'Do not join any of them, they are all corrupt.' The vision then ended."

From the BYU version, *The Wentworth Letter*, on page 296, we read: ". . . I was enwrapped in a heavenly vision and saw two glorious personages who exactly resembled each other in features, and likeness, surrounded with a brilliant light which eclipsed the sun at noon-day." However, instead of only the Lord instructing Joseph, we read: "*They told me* that all religious denominations were believing in incorrect doctrines, and that none of them was acknowledged of God as his church and kingdom" (Italics added).

Though the following information is not related in any of the versions, it is worth quoting what Elder B. H. Roberts said: "He saw a pillar of light descending from heaven—it rested upon him—its brightness exceeded the brightness of the sun at noon-day. In the midst of this glorious light stood two personages; each resembling the other. *One standing a little above the other*, pointing to the *one below him* said: 'This is my beloved son, hear ye him.'"[36]

It appears consistent that the Father, who is the greatest of all, would stand slightly above our Lord, and give direction to the boy-prophet. While living in mortality, Jesus said to his apostles, "I go unto the Father: for my Father is greater than I" (John 14:28). Though Jesus is a God, he is also the Son of God;

therefore, the Father is his God as he is ours. For as the risen Lord told Mary Magdalene, "I ascend unto my Father, and your Father; and to my God, and your God" (John 20:17).

Returning to the official version, we are given further information concerning what Jesus told Joseph: "I was answered that I must join none of them [sects of religion], for they were all wrong; and the Personage who addressed me said that all their creeds were an abomination in his sight; that those professors were all corrupt; that: 'they draw near me with their lips, but their hearts are far from me, they teach the doctrines the commandments of men, having a form of godliness, but they deny the power thereof.'"

Concluding his remarks concerning this glorious vision, Joseph simply says in the official version: "He again forbade me to join any of them; and many other things did he say unto me, which I cannot write at this time." Then, he tells what happened to him when the vision ended: "When I came to myself again, I found myself lying on my back, looking up into heaven. When the light had departed, I had no strength; but soon recovering in some degree, I went home" (Joseph Smith—History 1:19-20).

As is apparent, there are differences in these various accounts. However, it is important to point out that each compliment and supplement the official version.

Though there are different versions, millions of individuals—including this author—have prayed to the Father, in the name of the Son, and received a spiritual confirmation from the Holy Ghost that the Father and the Son appeared to Joseph Smith, Jr. in the Sacred Grove, on a beautiful, clear day, early in the spring of

1820. Further, that Joseph is a prophet, and the head of this the final dispensation of time. Regarding this marvelous vision, we conclude by using the words of the Lord's anointed:

" . . . I had actually seen a light, and in the midst of that light I saw two Personages, and they did in reality speak to me; and though I was hated and persecuted for saying that I had seen a vision, *yet it was true*;

"I knew it, and I knew that God knew it, and I could not deny it, neither dared I do it; at least I knew that by so doing I would offend God, and come under condemnation" (Joseph Smith—History 1:25) (Italics added).

CHAPTER FOUR
DOCTRINES LEARNED FROM THE FIRST VISION

DOCTRINES CONCERNING THE FATHER AND SON

In the Prophet Joseph's time there were many teachings concerning the Godhead. We shall only consider a few of these: Many people believed that the members of the Godhead—the Father, Son, and Holy Ghost—were one in the same person. Various preachers believed and taught that God no longer communicated with mankind. In addition, they believed that God did not have a physical body, but was a Spirit that was everywhere present. Besides these teachings, several taught that visions and revelations had ceased.

Continuing with the official version, we discover that after Joseph entered the family home, he did not immediately tell any member he had seen the Father or the Son in the grove. He says: "And as I leaned up to the fireplace, mother inquired what the matter was. I replied, 'Never mind, all is well—I am well enough off.'" After a short pause, he told his mother, "I have learned for myself that Presbyterianism is not true" (Joseph Smith—History 1:20).

As we will recall, the Lord told young Joseph not to join with any religion; "*and many other things did he say unto me, which I cannot write at this time*" (Joseph Smith—History 1:20) (Italics added). Though we are not

31

told, we may properly believe that the Lord instructed Joseph to tell what he had seen and heard, but in his telling to use wisdom—even with his immediate family. In support of this theory, we turn to the account of the premortal Lord appearing to the brother of Jared on the top of a mountain. During this glorious vision, the "Lord said unto [this man]: Behold, thou shalt not suffer these things which ye have seen and heard to go forth unto the world, until the time cometh that I shall glorify my name in the flesh; wherefore, ye shall treasure up the things which ye have seen and heard, and show it to no man" (Ether 3:21). The Lord then instructed this righteous man that he should write the vision, and in due time, with the aid of two stones, they would "magnify to the eyes of men these things which ye shall write" (Ether 22-24).

The opposite instruction seems to be the case with Joseph, for he says: "Some few days after I had this vision, I happened to be in company with one of the Methodist preachers, who was very active in the before mentioned religious excitement; and, conversing with him on the subject of religion, *I took occasion to give an account of the vision which I had had*" (Joseph Smith—History 1:21) (Italics added).

Concerning his reaction, the boy-prophet explains: "I was greatly surprised at his behavior; he treated my communications not only lightly, but with great contempt, saying it was all of the devil, that there were no such things as visions or revelations in these days; that all such things had ceased with the apostles, and that there would never be any more of them" (Joseph Smith—History 1:21).

In stark contrast from what this preacher said that

revelations and visions had ceased, the Prophet solemnly declares, "For I had seen a vision; I knew it, and I knew that God knew it, and I could not deny it . . . " (Joseph Smith—History 1:25). Concerning this glorious vision, we use the words of President Heber J. Grant: "The vision was a reality and direct. When Joseph received it, men were loath [reluctant] to believe that it was possible for God or holy beings to speak to man on the earth . . ."[37]

It is important to understand that this vision was not even a vision in the sense we normally speak of visions. The Father and his Son appeared to the Prophet Joseph Smith literally and physically. They individually and collectively spoke with the boy-prophet and gave him important instructions. With this knowledge, we turn our attention to doctrines learned concerning the Father and the Son.

From the BYU version of the First Vision on page 296, we find that Joseph saw "two glorious personages who exactly resembled each other in features and likeness." In addition, they were "surrounded with a brilliant light which eclipsed the sun at noon-day."

PHYSICAL ATTRIBUTES
OF THE FATHER AND SON

In describing the physical attributes of the Father—which equally apply to the Son—President George Q. Cannon, First Counselor to President John Taylor, said: "Joseph saw that the Father had a form; that He had a head; that He had arms; that He had limbs; that He had feet; that He had a face and a tongue with which to express His thoughts; for He said unto Joseph: 'This is my beloved Son'—pointing to the Son—'hear Him.'"[38]

Previous to this description, President Brigham Young stated: "We differ from them [other religions] in our ideas of God. We know that he is a Being—a man— with all the component parts of an intelligent being—head, hair, eyes, ears, nose, mouth, cheek bones, forehead, chin, body, lower limbs; *that he eats, drinks*, talks, lives and has a being [body], and has a residence . . ."[39] (Italics added).

Regarding President Young's comment that God eats and drinks, Elder Joseph Fielding Smith, in 1936, said this in General Conference: "I heard of one man . . . who made the statement, as the report comes to me, . . . that we shall have to cease believing in the anthropomorphic God [described as having a human form or human attributes]; we must quit thinking of God as being in the form in which man is made. He ridiculed the idea by saying, 'Can we worship a God who has to eat, who has to sleep, who has to take a bath?' Of course, in thinking of God as a person in whose image we are created, we do not necessarily have to think of him as having to conform to all the conditions of mortal existence to which we, under present conditions, are forced to subscribe. *But is there anything wrong in thinking of a God who eats?* He did eat and has promised to eat again. What is wrong in it? *He bathes, at least in fire*, so he tells us. We are his off-spring, and he has given us commandments to serve him in the name of his Only Begotten Son as sons and daughters unto God."[40]

Therefore, the Prophet was able to see that the Father and his Son were separate, glorified men, who had physical bodies identical in form to mortal man. In addition, these two Personages were able to move and verbally communicate to him in his own language.

"STANDING ABOVE ME IN THE AIR"

We now turn our attention to the official version of the First Vision, wherein the Prophet says, "I saw two Personages . . . *standing above me in the air*" (Joseph Smith—History 1:17) (Italics added). With this knowledge, we discover that gravity, as we know it, does not have the same force and influence on resurrected beings as it does mortals. To help better understand the ability of the Father and the Son to stand in the air, Elder Orson Pratt wrote: "Man has legs, so has God . . . Man walks with his legs, so does God sometimes . . . God can not only walk, *but he can move up and down through the air without using his legs as in the process of walking . . .* God, though in the figure of a man, has many powers that man has not got. He can go upwards through the air. He can waft [move] himself from world to world by his own self-moving powers. These are powers not possessed by man only through faith, as in the instances of Enoch and Elijah. Therefore, though in the figure of a man, *he has powers far superior to man*"[41] (Italics added).

HOW JOSEPH WAS ABLE
TO SEE THE FATHER AND SON

Many people have wondered if the Prophet saw the Father and the Son with his natural eyes or his spiritual eyes. To answer this question, we use the words of Elder Spencer W. Kimball. He wrote: "Moses declares 'he saw God face to face, and he talked with him . . . ' (Moses 1:2).

"This experience with Moses is in harmony with the scripture that says:

"'For no man has seen God at any time in the flesh, *except quickened by the Spirit of God.*

"'Neither can any natural man abide the presence of God, neither after the carnal mind' (D&C 67:11-12).

"It must be obvious, then, that to endure the glory of the Father or the glorified Christ, a mortal being must be *translated or otherwise fortified.*

"Grease on the swimmer's body or a heavy rubber skin diver's suit may protect one from cold and wet; an asbestos suit might protect a firefighter from flames; a bullet-proof vest may save one from assassin's bullets; one's heated home may protect from winter's chilling blasts; deep shade or smoked glass can modify the withering heat and burning rays of the midday sun. *There is a protective force that God brings into play when he exposes his human servants to the glories of his person and his works.*" Later, he wrote, "When properly protected with the glory of God, and when sufficiently perfected, *man can see God*"[42] (Italics added).

With another understanding, Elder Joseph Fielding Smith has written: "We may after baptism and confirmation become companions of the Holy Ghost who will teach us the ways of the Lord, quicken our minds and help us to understand the truth. The people of the world do not receive the gift of the Holy Ghost.

"Joseph Smith did not have the gift of the Holy Ghost at the time of the First Vision, but he was overshadowed by the Holy Ghost; otherwise, he could not have beheld the Father and the Son."[43] (Italics added)

In addition to being translated or fortified with a protective force, or being overshadowed by the Holy Ghost, we discover another way that Joseph was able to see God. As Elder McConkie has written: "Jesus said:

36

'Blessed are the pure in heart: for they shall see God' (Matt. 5:8), meaning that every person who perfects his life shall see God, here and now, while he yet dwells in the flesh, and that if he continues in grace, he shall also see and dwell with him everlastingly in the realms of immortal glory.

"*As revealed to Joseph Smith*, the divine law enabling man to see Deity is couched in these words: 'Verily, thus saith the Lord: It shall come to pass that every soul who forsaketh his sins and cometh unto me, and calleth on my name, and obeying my voice, and keepeth my commandments, shall see my face and know that I am'"[44] (D&C 93:1) (Italics added).

From the BYU version on page 284, we are informed that when the Lord appeared, "he said unto [Joseph] thy sins are forgiven given thee." At that moment in time, this young man had forsaken his sins, was in the process of calling on the Lord for an answer, and was willing to obey the Lord's voice. Therefore, according to the divine law as stated by Elder McConkie, Joseph Smith, Jr. was able to see the face of the Lord.

Based upon what is written in the 84th section of the Doctrine and Covenants, various people have wondered how Joseph was able to see the Father and his Son in 1820, when he was not yet ordained to the Melchizedek Priesthood. To answer this question, we turn to the writings of Elder Orson F. Whitney in 1913. His introduction reads: "SPIRITS FOREORDAINED." Then, these explanatory words are written:

"In view of the fact that these ordinations [to the Aaronic and Melchizedek Priesthoods] were subsequent to the Prophet's vision, in the spring of 1820, when the Father and the Son appeared to him, *some have found it difficult to interpret the divine declaration, that no man without the Melchizedek Priesthood 'can see the face of God, even the Father, and live'* (D&C 84:19-22). But the problem is easy of solution, in the light of the Prophet's teachings. Did he not give the key to it when he said that certain men, called to minister to the inhabitants of this world, *were ordained to that very purpose before the world was?*

". . . For if no man without the Melchizedek Priesthood can see the face of God the Father and live, and Joseph Smith, nine years before he received either of the Priesthoods from those heavenly messengers, looked upon the faces of both the Father and the Son and survived, it indicates, in accordance with his own statement . . . that certain spirits are ordained to certain callings before they tabernacle in the flesh, *and that he himself held the Melchizedek Priesthood when he saw the face of God at the opening of the last gospel dispensation . . .* "[45] (Italics added).

Eight years earlier in a General Conference, Elder Whitney spoke on this same subject, but added information that President Lorenzo Snow had told him: "It is said that without the Melchizedek Priesthood no man can look upon the face of God and live. And yet, Joseph Smith, when a boy of fourteen years, gazed upon the Father and the Son, *and it was nine years before he held the Priesthood in the flesh.* I once asked President Lorenzo Snow concerning this matter: 'Why is it, if a man without the Melchizedek Priesthood cannot look upon God's face and live, that Joseph Smith could see the Father and the Son, and live, when he held no priesthood at all?' *President Snow replied: 'Joseph did hold the priesthood; he came with it into the world.'* I believed it before he said it, but I wanted him to say it first. Joseph Smith, as much as any Prophet that ever lived, was ordained a prophet before he came into this mortal life. *He held the Melchizedek Priesthood in the spirit, when he came here* [to earth], or he could never have received what he did from God"[46] (Italics added).

In a personal letter dated January 3, 1947, Elder Joseph Fielding Smith wrote that "President Lorenzo Snow said that Joseph Smith could see God because of the power of the Priesthood which he held before he came here. Without any doubt men chosen to positions of trust in the spirit world, held priesthood."[47]

Also in a personal letter dated February 20, 1881, his father, Joseph F. Smith, of the First Presidency at the time wrote: "Joseph Smith held the Melchizedek Priesthood before he came to the earth—as did Jesus— but it had to be *reconfirmed upon him in the flesh* by Peter, James and John, as upon Jesus by Moses and Elias on the Mount . . . "[49] (Italics added).

From what has been presented, we discover that there are at least four ways that Joseph Smith, Jr. was able to see the Father and the Son. Therefore, in the spring of 1820, as Elder Joseph Fielding Smith has appropriately written: " . . . after the vision was given to Joseph Smith of the Father and the Son, *he stood the only witness among men who could testify with knowledge that God lives and Jesus Christ is verily his Son.* In this knowledge he became *a special witness for Christ,* and thus *an apostle before the Priesthood had been restored* . . . "[49] (Italics added).

CONCLUSION

The doctrines that Joseph learned concerning the Father and the Son are as follows: They are separate, glorified men, who have physical bodies similar in form to mortal man. He observed that they exactly resembled each other in features and likeness. Each had the ability to stand in the air as easily as if they were on solid ground. Individually and collectively, they were able to verbally communicate to him in his native language. Because He knew him, the Father personally called Joseph by name, but did not instruct him, but told the boy-prophet to receive instruction from his beloved Son. Our Lord, not the Father, said to him, "Thy sins are forgiven thee." Therefore, according to divine law, the boy-prophet had forsaken his sins, making him worthy to be in their presence and see their face (See D&C 93:1).

Joseph also discovered that Satan had no power or influence over him when these Supreme Beings appeared in celestial fire. The boy-prophet observed that the leaves of the trees were not consumed by their brightness and glory. When this glorious vision ended, and the Father and the Son had departed, Joseph experienced that he did not have his normal, physical strength, but was soon able to regain it. Therefore, as Elder Joseph Fielding Smith has written, he was the only witness who could testify with knowledge that God lives and Jesus Christ is verily his Son. Thereby, he became a special witness for Christ, and thus an apostle before the Priesthood was restored.

CHAPTER FIVE
MORONI APPEARS TO JOSEPH

MORONI'S FIRST VISIT

After Joseph left the grove of trees in the spring of 1820, he says that for over three years he continued to pursue his common vocations in life with no heavenly communication during that time-frame. True to his word that he had seen both the Father and the Son, the boy prophet says, ". . . all the time suffering severe persecution at the hands of all classes of men, both religious and irreligious, *because I continued to affirm that I had seen a vision*" (Joseph Smith—History 1:27) (Italics added).

Being young and inexperienced in the ways of the world, he openly confesses, "I was left to all kinds of temptations; and, mingling with all kinds of society, I frequently fell into many foolish errors, *and displayed the weakness of youth*, and the foibles [minor flaw in character] of human nature; which, I am sorry to say, led me into divers temptations, offensive in the sight of God." Being quick to clarify this statement, he says, "In making this confession, no one need suppose me guilty of any great or malignant sins. A disposition to commit such was never in my nature. But I was guilty of levity, and sometimes associated with jovial company . . . not consistent with that character which ought to be maintained by one *who was called of God as I had been*. But this will not seem very strange to any one who recollects my youth, and is acquainted with *my native cheery temperament*" (Joseph Smith—History 1:28) (Italics added).

At age seventeen, Joseph declares that on the evening of September 21, 1823, after retiring to his bed for the night, *he supplicated the Lord in earnest prayer for forgiveness of all of his sins and follies.* Not having received a heavenly communication for over three years, he asked for a manifestation to know of his state and standing with God. With firm and active faith, he explains, "*For I had full confidence in obtaining a divine manifestation,* as I previously had one" [Meaning: The First Vision] (Joseph Smith—History 1:29) (Italics added).

While praying, Joseph discovered a light appearing in his room, which continued to increase until the room was lighter than at noonday, when immediately a personage appeared at his bedside, standing in the air, for his feet did not touch the floor (Joseph Smith—History 1:30). Whether or not other sibling brothers were asleep in the same room, we are not informed. If they were present, this heavenly manifestation—by divine laws not understood or revealed—did not disturb their slumber in any degree.

Just as the Father and the Son appeared to young Joseph in a glorious light, so did this heavenly being. During the First Vision, the two Personages were standing in the air; likewise, this singular person did the same.

Continuing his description, Joseph says that this individual "*had on a loose robe of most exquisite white-ness.* It was whiteness beyond anything earthly I had ever seen; nor do I believe that any earthly thing could be made to appear so exceedingly white and brilliant" (Joseph Smith—History 1:31) (Italics added).

The reader is informed that none of the First Vision accounts describe the clothing that the Father and the Son were wearing. Now that Joseph was three years older, he was more observant and descriptive about the appearance of this glorious being.

"His hands were naked, and his arms also, a little above the wrist; so, also, were his feet naked, as were his legs, a little above his ankles. His head and neck were also bare. I could discover that he had no other clothing on but this robe, as it was open, so that I could see into his bosom.

"Not only was his robe exceedingly white, but his whole person was glorious beyond description, and his countenance truly like lightning. *The room was exceedingly light, but not so very bright as immediately around his person*" (Joseph Smith—History 1:31-32) (Italics added). Therefore, we find that this glorious light did not come from above this visitor, but radiated from his person, and this light became less brilliant the farther it was from him. Though this individual's countenance was bright like lightning, it did not blind the eyes of Joseph, and he was able to clearly see this radiant being.

Startled by this illuminating personage, the boy-prophet reveals, "When I first looked upon him, *I was afraid*; but the fear soon left me" (Joseph Smith—History 1:32) (Italics added). Evidently, Joseph rapidly knew by the Spirit that this appearance was not of the devil, but was an angelic manifestation. Accordingly, his fear quickly left him and he felt calm and peaceful.

Just as it transpired in the grove of trees three years

previously, wherein God the Father called Joseph by name, this radiant personage did likewise. "He called me by name, and said unto me that he was a messenger sent from the presence of God to me, and *that his name was Moroni*; that *God had a work for me to do*; and that my name should be had for good and evil among all nations, kindreds, tongues and people, or that it should be both good and evil spoken among all people." To himself, Joseph probably wondered what work God wanted him to do? Continuing, he explains, "[Moroni] said there was a book deposited, written upon gold plates giving an account of the former inhabitants of this continent, and the source from whence they sprang. He also said that the fulness of the everlasting Gospel was contained in it, as delivered by the Savior to the ancient inhabitants; Also, that there were two stones in silver bows—and these stones, fastened to a breastplate, constituted what is called the Urim and Thummim—deposited with the plates; and the possession and use of these stones were what constituted 'seers' in ancient or former times; and that God had prepared them for the purpose of translating the book" (Joseph Smith—History 1:33-35) (Italics added).

Seven years in the future, Joseph would discover from translating the gold plates that the *Angel Moroni* was the last of the Nephite prophets who had charge of the records from which the *Book of Mormon* was translated. How fitting that this ancient, record-keeper would introduce this "book," and tutor this young man to become a mighty prophet for the last and final dispensation.

From a writing titled *Details of Moroni's Visit Prove Joseph A Prophet*, Elder Joseph Fielding Smith says that when Moroni first appeared on the night of September 21, 1823, this "angel quoted to the young man, Joseph Smith, part of the third and all of the fourth chapters of Malachi, with some variations from the reading as we find it in the King James translation of the *Bible*.

"He also quoted the 11th chapter of Isaiah, saying that it was about to be fulfilled; also the 22nd and 23rd verses of the third chapter of Acts, and the second chapter of Joel, verses 28 to the end, which he said were shortly to be fulfilled. He also said that the time for the fulness of the gentiles would soon come in, and many other scriptures were quoted which pertain to the dispensation of the fulness of times . . .

"The significance of this statement coming from Joseph Smith is the *frankness* with which he has given to the world, presenting chapters and verses in definite order, with the declaration that the time is at hand for their fulfillment.

"How would he dare to make such a statement, if the presentation of it was only imagination, or a falsehood presented to deceive? He would know that if this information was not given by the angel it surely would be proved untrue, for the promised fulfillment of the predictions would not come to pass.

"Joseph Smith, then but a boy, did not have the knowledge of the times by which he could of himself make such predictions. In fact, the learned men of the world could not make such predictions in that day, for they also were without the power of discernment and could not read the signs of the times. The fact that some of the words of Moroni to Joseph Smith have been fulfilled, and that others are now being fulfilled, lends credence to the fact that this young man spoke the truth, as he received it from a messenger sent from the presence of the Lord"⁵⁰ (Italics in quotation).

It is worth pointing out that Joseph did not tell all, or was instructed not to tell all, that Moroni told him that first visit. For Joseph says, "He quoted many other passages of scripture, and offered many explanations which cannot be mentioned here" (Joseph Smith—History 1:41). Giving specific instructions, Moroni told the boy-prophet, "that when [he] got those plates of which he had spoken—for the time that they should be obtained was not yet fulfilled—[he] should not show them to any person; neither the breastplate with the Urim and Thummim; only to those to whom I should be commanded to show them; *if I did I should be destroyed*" (Joseph Smith—History 1:42) (Italics added).

VISION OF WHERE THE PLATES WERE DEPOSITED

Continuing his narrative, Joseph says that while Moroni "was conversing with me about the plates, *the vision was opened to my mind* that I could see the place where the plates were deposited, and that so clearly and distinctly that I knew the place again when I visited it" (Joseph Smith—History 1:42) (Italics added).

Though many have classified Moroni's appearance as a vision, we notice the difference between the actual visit by this heavenly messenger and the vision that Joseph was shown where the plates were. To help clarify these differences, we use the words of Elder Wilford Woodruff. "Then, again, there are visions. Paul, you know, on one occasion was caught up to the third heaven and saw things that were not lawful to utter. He did not know whether he was in the body or out of it. That was a vision. When Joseph Smith, however, was visited by Moroni and the apostles, it was not particularly a vision which he had; he talked with them face to face."⁵¹

Continuing with Joseph's narrative, Joseph says: "After this communication, I saw the light in the room begin to gather immediately around the person of him who had been speaking to me, and it continued to do so until the room was again left dark, except just around him; when, instantly I saw, as it were, a conduit open right up into heaven, and he ascended till he entirely disappeared, and the room was left as it had been before this heavenly light had made its appearance" (Joseph Smith—History 1:43).

Similar to how a dimmer is used in our day, we are informed that the radiant light that filled the bedroom was dramatically dimmed, or as Joseph says, was gathered immediately around this heavenly messenger until "the room was again left dark, except just around him." Then, without saying a word, Moroni ascended silently and effortlessly out of Joseph's sight.

MORONI'S SECOND VISIT

While lying on his bed marveling over all that had transpired, Joseph says, "I suddenly discovered that my room was again beginning to get lighted, and in an instant, as it were, the same heavenly messenger was again by my bedside.

"He commenced, and again related the very same things which he had done at his first visit, *without the least variation . . .*" (Joseph Smith—History 1:44-45) (Italics added).

The tutoring of a prophet had commenced in earnest. Now that he was three years older, Joseph was able to receive further light and knowledge from heaven. To help the boy-prophet remember important instructions, Moroni repeats his teachings, without any variation. *Then, the messenger "informed [Joseph] of great judgments which were coming upon the earth,* with great desolations by famine, sword, and pestilence; and that these grievous judgments would come on the earth in this generation." After these words were spoken, Moroni "again ascended as he had done before" (Joseph Smith—History 1:45).

MORONI'S THIRD VISIT

"By this time, so deep were the impressions made on my mind," says Joseph, "that sleep had fled from my eyes, and I lay overwhelmed in astonishment at what I had both seen and heard. But what was my surprise when again I beheld the same messenger at my bedside, and heard him rehearse or repeat over again to me the same things as before; *and added a caution to me, telling me that Satan would try to tempt me* (in consequence of the indigent [financially poor] circumstances of my father's family), *to get the plates for the purpose of getting rich.* This he forbade me, saying that I must have no other object in view in getting the plates but to glorify God, and must not be influenced by any other motive than that of building his kingdom; *otherwise I could not get them*" (Joseph Smith—History 1:46) (Italics added).

It is a truism that repetition is the law of retention.

Three times Moroni appeared to the boy-prophet and gave him identical instructions. However, on the second and third visits, this heavenly messenger spoke of pending judgments that would come on the earth, and gave Joseph specific instructions concerning the plates.

"After this third visit, [Moroni] again ascended into heaven as before, and [Joseph] was again left to ponder on the strangeness of what [he] had just experienced." To his surprise, Joseph says, ". . . almost immediately after the heavenly messenger had ascended from me for the third time, the cock crowed, and I found that day was approaching, so that our interviews must have occupied the whole of that night" (Joseph Smith—History 1:47).

Prior to Moroni's first visit, we are not informed by Joseph of the time that he went to his bedroom to retire for the night. Nor do we know what time the rooster announced that morning was approaching. As such, we have no information of how many hours were involved in these instructional appearances. Whatever time-frame was involved, Joseph did not obtain any sleep.

MORONI'S FOURTH VISIT

Following these glorious visits throughout the night, the boy-prophet tells what happened in the morning. He says that he arose from his bed, "as usual, went to the necessary labors of the day; but, in attempting to work as at other times, *I found that my strength so exhausted as to render me entirely unable.* My father, who was laboring along with me, discovered something to be wrong with me, and told me to go home. I started with the intention of going to the house; but, in attempting to cross the fence out of the field where we were, *my*

49

strength entirely failed me, and I fell helpless to the ground, and for a time was quite unconscious of anything" (Joseph Smith—History 1:48) (Italics added).

As we may recall, after the First Vision had ended and the light disappeared, the boy-prophet says, "I had no strength; but soon recovering in some degree, I went home" (Joseph Smith—History 1:20). Concerning the visits by Moroni, there are two apparent reasons for Joseph's strength failing him. 1) The boy-prophet says that his interviews with the heavenly messenger must have occupied the whole of that night; therefore, lack of sleep caused him to fall unconscious (Joseph Smith—History 1:47). 2) These divine appearances caused his normal strength to be drained of its normal ability. In support of this statement, we turn to the experience of Moses when he spoke face to face with God. Later, when the presence of God withdrew from this mighty prophet and he was left unto himself, he fell back to the earth. "And it came to pass that *it was for the space of many hours before Moses did again receive his natural strength like unto man;* and he said unto himself: Now, for this cause I know that man is nothing, which thing I never had supposed" (Moses 1:9-10) (Italics added).

Returning to his narrative, the boy-prophet says: "The first thing that I can recollect was a voice speaking unto me, calling me by name. I looked up, and beheld the same messenger standing over my head, surrounded by light as before. He then again related unto me all that he had related to me the previous night, *and commanded me to go to my father and tell him of the vision and commandments which I had received*" (Joseph Smith—History 1:49) (Italics added).

Regarding Moroni's commandment for Joseph to go

and tell his father of the vision and commandments he had received, we turn to the *History of Joseph Smith*, by his mother, Lucy Mack Smith, to obtain this additional information. Joseph's mother says that "when the messenger whom he saw the previous night, visited him again, and the first thing he said was, '*Why did you not tell your father that which I commanded you to tell him?*' Joseph replied, '*I was afraid my father would not believe me.*' The angel rejoined, '*He will believe every word you say to him.*'

"Joseph then promised the angel that he would do as he had been commanded. Upon this, the messenger departed, and Joseph returned to the field, where he had left my husband and Alvin; but when he got there, his father had just gone to the house as he was somewhat unwell. Joseph then desired Alvin to go straightway and see his father and inform him that he had something of great importance to communicate to him, and that he wanted him to come out into the field where they were at work. Alvin did as he requested, and when my husband got there, *Joseph related to him all that had passed between him and the angel the previous night and that morning. Having heard this account, his father charged him not to fail in attending strictly to the instruction which he had received from this heavenly messenger*"[52] (Italics added).

Just as there are various accounts of the First Vision, we find out that there is another version of Joseph's History, which was originally dictated by his mother in 1845. With the approval of President Brigham Young, shortly after 1865 this History was carefully revised and checked for accuracy by President George A. Smith and Judge Elias Smith, who were cousins of the Prophet.

The reader is reminded that the *History of Joseph Smith* by his Mother, Lucy Mack Smith, supplements and compliments the Prophet's history. We are most grateful that additional information has been given of sacred events that transpired September 21-22, 1823.

Concerning appearances by the messenger to the boy-prophet, we use the inspired words of President J. Reuben Clark: "Some three years after the great vision in the woods, a heavenly messenger, Moroni, came to Joseph, now almost eighteen years old, and began instructing him in the duties of the great mission that had been given to him. *The instructions came gradually, for his mind was finite*, while *the subject was infinite*. So, as time went on, God revealed to the boy prophet the things he should know in order to restore and again build up the Church of Christ on earth . . ."[53] (Italics added).

Concluding our study of Moroni appearing to Joseph, it is apparent that the tutoring of a prophet had commenced in earnest. Being three years older from the time that the glorious First Vision happened, the boy prophet was mentally and spiritually ready to receive further light and knowledge from heaven. So that Joseph would remember important instructions, the heavenly messenger appeared four times in a short span of time and repeated the same message. However, after the first visit the boy-prophet was given additional information at each appearance by the angel.

CHAPTER SIX
THE HILL CUMORAH
FOUR YEARLY VISITS TO THE HILL

From the official version, we learn what Joseph did after the angel told him to tell his father: "I returned to my father in the field, and rehearsed the whole matter to him. He replied to me that it was of God, and told me to go and do as commanded by the messenger" (Joseph Smith—History 1:50).

Speaking of fathers in our day, Elder Boyd K. Packer has given this wise counsel: ". . . he taught the missionaries to discontinue teaching families unless or until, one—you have every father present, or two—you've made every reasonable effort to get him. Why? Because this is the church that puts families together, *not the one that pulls them apart*"⁵⁴ (Italics added). Such was the case with Joseph Smith, Jr. and his immediate family.

From one of the stories in the *Book of Mormon*, we read that Nephi had broken his bow, which was made of fine steel. After his bow was broken, he was not able to obtain food for the families who were traveling toward a promised land. The record further states that his brothers, "Laman and Lemuel and the sons of Ishmael did begin to murmur exceedingly, because of their sufferings and afflictions in the wilderness; *and also my father began to murmur against the Lord his God*; yea, and they were all exceedingly sorrowful, even that they did murmur against the Lord" (1 Nephi 16:18-20) (Italics added).

After this righteous man, Nephi, had spoken many words unto his brethren, he "did make out of wood a bow, and out of a straight stick, an arrow; wherefore, I did arm myself with a bow and an arrow, with a sling and with stones. *And I said unto my father: Whither shall I go to obtain food?*

"And it came to pass that he [Lehi] did inquire of the Lord, for they [he, his sons, and the sons of Ishmael] had humbled themselves because of my words; for I did say many things unto them in the energy of my soul" (1 Nephi 16:22-24) (Italics added).

This same record informs us that Lehi was a prophet. However, at this particular time of hardship, he began to murmur against the Lord. Because Nephi respected his father as the head of the household and as a prophet, this righteous son sought Lehi's support and counsel of where to go to obtain food.

Though the Prophet Joseph personally saw the Father and the Son and had recently received four heavenly communications from Moroni, this righteous son was "commanded" by this angel to speak with his earthly father. Why? It was vitally important for the head of the Smith household, Joseph Smith, Sr., to give support and counsel to the head of the final dispensation, Joseph Smith, Jr., "to go and do as commanded by the messenger" (Joseph Smith—History 1:50). Because of these glorious appearances, persecution and trials would increase in their lives, and it was absolutely necessary that the Smith family remain together, not pulled apart.

Returning to Joseph's narrative, wherein he went to the Hill Cumorah, we find from the instruction previously given by the messenger and the distinctness of the vision which he had concerning it, the boy-prophet immediately knew the place the moment he arrived there (Joseph Smith—History 1:50). As to where this *place* was, we read the following description by the boy prophet: "Convenient to the village of Manchester, Ontario county, New York, stands a hill of considerable size, and the most elevated of any in the neighborhood . . ." (Joseph Smith—History 1:51).

Oliver Cowdery, who later on would become a scribe for the Prophet Joseph Smith, gives this description: " . . . about four miles from Palmyra, you pass a large hill on the east side of the road. Why I say large, is because it is as large perhaps, as any in that country . . . I think I am justified in saying that this is the highest hill for some distance round, and I am certain that its appearance, as it rises so suddenly from the plain on the north, must attract the notice of the traveler as he passes by."[55]

LOCATION OF THE HILL CUMORAH

Though the Prophet Joseph Smith has stated that the Hill Cumorah is located near Manchester, New York, there are various people who believe that this hill is actually located outside of the United States. Regarding this thinking, Elder Joseph Fielding Smith says: "Within recent years there has arisen among certain students of the *Book of Mormon* a theory to the effect that within the period covered by the *Book of Mormon*, the Nephites and Lamanites were confined almost entirely within the borders of the territory comprising Central America and the southern portion of Mexico—the isthmus of Tehauntepec probably the "narrow neck' of land spoken of in the *Book of Mormon* rather than the isthmus of Panama.

"This *theory* is founded upon the assumption that it was impossible for the colony of Lehi to multiply and fill the hemisphere within the limits of 1,000 years, or from the coming of Lehi from Jerusalem to the time of the destruction of the Nephites at the Hill Cumorah." Likewise, they further say, that "migrations, building of cities, and the wars and contentions, preclude the possibility of the people spreading over great distances . . ."[56] (Italics added).

It needs to be emphasized that this type of thinking has been circulated and promoted for nearly fifty years. Various writings have been published to prove this theory. In these publications, various authors use geological data and photographs to support their claim. "Because of this theory," says Elder Joseph Fielding Smith, "some members of the Church have become confused and greatly disturbed in their faith in the *Book of Mormon*."[57]

IDENTIFYING CUMORAH, RAMAH, AND RIPLIANCUM

In writing of the final destruction of the Jaredite civilization, the prophet Ether explains that when Coriantumr, the king, saw that he and his people were about to fall, they fled before Shiz and his people and pitched their tents by "the waters of *Ripliancum*, which, by interpretation, *is large, or to exceed all.*" Soon, Shiz and his people also pitched their tents near them (Ether 15:7-8) (Italics added).

The following morning a great battle raged, and the people of Shiz fled southward to a place called Ogath. In this region was a hill known as *Ramah* (Ether 15:8-11) (Italics added).

Though it is sad to think of it as a last, great battle field, yet it is highly interesting to discover that the Hill Cumorah where the Nephites were destroyed is the same hill where the Jaredites were also destroyed. When the great compiler, Mormon, was abridging Ether's record, he wrote this revealing information: "And it came to pass that the army of Coriantumr did pitch their tents *by the Hill Ramah; and it was that same hill where my father Mormon did hide up the records unto the Lord,* which were sacred" (Ether 15:11) (Italics added).

Our attention is now turned to the description written by Mormon of the destruction of his people, the Nephite civilization. Identifying the same landmarks as written by Ether, but using a different name, he says: "And it came to pass that we did march forth to the land of Cumorah, and we did pitch our tents round about the *hill Cumorah*; and it was in a *land of many waters, rivers, and fountains*; and here we had hope to gain advantage over the Lamanites" (Mormon 6:4) (Italics added).

Continuing his commentary about this last great battle, Mormon tells that when all of the Nephite people were gathered to the land of Cumorah, he knew that it would be the last struggle of his people. Being old, Mormon remembered the commandment of the Lord that the records should not fall into the hands of the Lamanites, for they would destroy them; therefore, he says, "I . . . *hid up in the hill Cumorah all the records which had been entrusted to me by the hand of the Lord, save it were these few plates which I gave unto my son Moroni*" (Mormon 6:6) (Italics added).

Though the Jaredites called the hill Ramah, the Nephites called it the hill *Cumorah*. The Jaredites called the large body of water *Ripliancum*; whereas, Mormon describes it as a land of many waters, rivers, and fountains.

As to where these places are located, we again use the words of Elder Joseph Fielding Smith: "It must be conceded that this description fits perfectly the land of Cumorah in New York, as it has been known since the visitation of Moroni to the Prophet Joseph Smith, for the hill is in the proximity of the Great Lakes and also in the land of many waters and fountains. Moreover, *the Prophet Joseph Smith, himself, is on record, definitely declaring the present hill called Cumorah to be the exact hill spoken of in the Book of Mormon*"[58] (History of the Church, Volume 2, pp. 79-80) (Italics in quotation).

Not only do we have the Prophet Joseph Smith's declaration, we have testimonies by early Church leaders, Oliver Cowdery, Brigham Young, Heber C. Kimball, Parley P. Pratt, Orson Pratt, and David Whitmer, who have affirmed that the hill near Palmyra, New York is the identical hill where Mormon and his son, Moroni, hid the records.[59]

"MORMON HILL"

We now advance to a time after the *Book of Mormon* was published and discover that individuals who lived near the Hill Cumorah also believed that this was the place where Joseph obtained the plates. In a *Young Woman's Journal*, dated 1898, it reads: "The readers of this Journal have heard much of the history of the Hill Cumorah, *or, as it is better know to those who live at its base, 'Mormon Hill.'* However, I venture to say that there are many ears eager to hear the lingering echoes of prophetic thunder from the place they so much revere.

"*Cumorah, to us, is what Sinai was to Israel.* From one came the tablets of stone engraved by the finger of God, *from the other we receive the metallic plates written by the pen of inspiration.* To stand on this memorable spot, where the celestial light was shown as from the burning bush, is like drawing a breath in paradise"[60] (Italics added).

This elegantly worded article adequately points out that those who lived at the base of the "Mormon Hill" identify it as the place where the plates were received by the Prophet Joseph Smith.

We now turn to another publication, *The Juvenile Instructor*, and learn of a different meaning for "Mormon Hill." The following article was printed in 1873. "While on a recent visit to the States on business, Brother Brigham Young, Jun. and the Editor of *The Juvenile Instructor* [who was Elder George Q. Cannon], arranged to make a visit to the hill Cumorah—*the hill where Mormon and Moroni secreted the records*, by the command of the Lord, which were revealed to the Prophet Joseph Smith, and from which he translated the *Book of Mormon* . . . We had proceeded a little over a mile on the road when the driver of the carriage pointed out a hill to us on our left, which he said *was 'Mormon Hill.'* We supposed that by this he meant Cumorah. Though in its general appearance it resembled the descriptions we had had of Cumorah, yet we were somewhat disappointed in its size, as it was not so high a hill as many others which we saw in the neighborhood. In fact, as we rode along, we saw several hills which we thought more like what we imagined Cumorah to be than the one pointed out to us. We rode on for probably two miles farther, conversing but very little and each absorbed in his own reflections, when we saw, immediately in front of us, a hill that rose suddenly, almost precipitously, from the plain. Brother Brigham, Jun., remarked when he saw it: 'There is a hill which agrees in appearance with my idea of Cumorah.' In this opinion the Editor coincided. The driver, hearing our remarks, turned to us and said: *'Yes, this is Gold Bible Hill.'* We asked him what he meant by calling the other, which he had pointed out to us, 'Mormon Hill.' He replied that there was a cave in that hill which the 'Mormons' had dug and some of them had lived in it, so the people said; and therefore, it was known by that name"[61] (Italics added).

In support of what was printed in the first publication of *Young Woman's Journal*, Brother Andrew Jenson in a General Conference in 1917 said, ". . . it is within the present boundaries of that mission that the so-called 'Mormon' hill, the Hill Cumorah is located."[62]

From these writings we find that the hill that the Prophet obtained the gold plates from has been referred to as "Gold Bible Hill," "Mormon Hill," and in our day, commonly called the "Hill Cumorah." Accordingly, those members of the Church who believe that Joseph Smith, Jr. is a prophet of God should discredit all people who theorize that the Hill Cumorah is located outside of the United States. As to where it is located, we conclude are study of its location by using the words of Joseph: "Convenient to the village of Manchester, Ontario county, New York, stands a hill of considerable size" (Joseph Smith—History 1:51).

JOSEPH VIEWS CONTENTS OF THE BOX

After leaving his father in the field, Joseph walked a distance of approximately three miles to this place that was shown in vision. Because the Lord and his Church respect the legal rights of ownership, we may properly suppose that no one owned this hill in 1823. As such, it was part of the undeveloped frontier that was located between Palmyra and Manchester in the western part of the state of New York.

We wonder what thoughts must have passed through the boy-prophet's mind as he journeyed to this place where the plates were deposited! Surely he must have rehearsed what Moroni had told him about the book, written upon gold plates, that was deposited there. Though Joseph does not inform us, we may safely assume that he had a mix of apprehensiveness and exciting feelings. After reaching the base of this hill, we may suppose that he rested for several minutes to regain his strength to ascend the hill. In describing the location of this depository, Joseph says that on the west side of this hill, not far from the top, under a stone of considerable size—that was thick and rounding in the middle on the upper side, and thinner towards the edge, which only the middle part was visible above the ground—lay the plates. Whether he used his hands or a rock nearby, the boy-prophet says that he removed the dirt around the stone. Then, having obtained a lever, which we may suppose was a branch from either a live or dead tree, Joseph, with a little exertion, removed the stone lid.

We can only imagine how this young man felt as he beheld the contents of this box which had been formed by laying stones together in some kind of cement. Inside, he beheld the *plates*, the *Urim and Thummim*, and the *breastplate*. Joseph says that he attempted to take the contents out of the box, but was forbidden by the messenger.

Paraphrasing another version by Oliver Cowdery, we discover that when Joseph tried to remove the plates, an unseen power sent a shock through him. Though he was startled and weakened by this power, he attempted two more times to remove the plates, but each time received stronger shocks. In frustration, he exclaimed audibly, "Why can I not obtain this book?" Thinking that he was alone, Joseph was startled at this response, "Because you have not kept the commandments of the Lord." Looking up, the boy-prophet once again saw Moroni and remembered that he, Joseph, had "failed to remember the great end for which [the plates] had been kept, and in consequence could not have power to take them."

This young man then began to pray and saw in vision the "prince of darkness" and his hosts, so he would "know hereafter the two powers and never be influenced or overcome by that wicked one."[63]

Returning to Joseph's History, we find that the messenger informed him again that the time for bringing forth the plates "had not yet arrived, neither would it, until four years from that time;" but he "should come to that place precisely in one year from that time." Moroni also told the boy-prophet that he would meet him each year and would continue to do so until Joseph received the plates (Joseph Smith—History 1:53) (Italics added).

In compliance with these instructions, Joseph says, "I went at the end of each year, and at each time I found the same messenger there, *and received instruction and intelligence from him at each of our interviews,* respecting what the Lord was going to do, and how and in what manner his kingdom was to be conducted in the last days" (Joseph Smith—History 1:54) (Italics added).

Though the Father and the Son had personally visited the boy-prophet in the grove of trees three years previously and had given him specific instruction, we observe with the appearances of Moroni an order establishing how further communications would come from the Father and the Son to Joseph Smith, Jr.—other heavenly messengers would eventually appear and give him instructions and keys.

CHAPTER SEVEN
JOSEPH OBTAINS THE PLATES

PREPARATORY YEARS

Though Joseph Smith, Jr. was foreordained to be the head of the final dispensation and brought with him all of the spiritual talents and abilities he had abundantly earned in the premortal existence, yet, even he had to mature spiritually, mentally, and physically in mortality so that he could perform the great work that he was called to do (See Joseph Smith—History 1:33-35).

The Father and the Son appeared to Joseph in the spring of 1820 at age 14. Over three years later, the Angel Moroni first appeared to the boy prophet on September 21, 1823, at age 17.

In addition to receiving instructions from this heavenly messenger, Joseph was shown a vision, which he does not mentioned in the official version. This information is obtained from *The Wentworth letter*, which was written by Joseph Smith, Jr. to a Mr. Wentworth, editor and proprietor of a newspaper called the *Chicago Democrat*. It was first published in the *Times and Seasons* of March 1, 1842 and is classified as one of the most inspired documents ever written by the Prophet Joseph Smith.

Telling what he saw in this vision, he writes: "I was also informed concerning the aboriginal inhabitants of this country *and shown who they were, and from whence they came*; a brief sketch of their origin, progress, civilization, laws, governments, of their right-eousness and iniquity, and the blessings of God being finally withdrawn from them as a people, was made known unto me . . ."[64] (Italics added).

By seeing in vision the ancient inhabitants of the American Continent, we readily learn how spiritually gifted Joseph was. It also adequately points out that he was called by the Lord to translate the record of this people.

Corroborating what the Prophet wrote to Mr. Wentworth, we turn to the history by his mother and read the following narrative: "The ensuing evening, when the family were together, Joseph made known to them all that he had communicated to his father in the field, and also of his finding the record, as well as what passed between him and the angel while he was at the place where the plates were deposited . . . by sunset the next day, we were all seated, and Joseph commenced telling us the great and glorious things which God had manifested to him; but, before proceeding, he charged us not to mention out of the family that which he was about to say to us, as the world was so wicked that when they came to a knowledge of these things they would try to take our lives; and that when he should obtain the plates, our names would be cast out as evil by all people. Hence the necessity of suppressing these things as much as possible, until the time should come for them to go forth to the world.

"From this time forth, Joseph continued to receive instructions from the Lord, and we continued to get the children together every evening for the purpose of listening while he gave us a relation of the same . . .

"*During our evening conversations, Joseph would*

occasionally give us some of the most amusing recitals that could be imagined. He would describe the ancient inhabitants of this continent, their dress, mode of traveling, and the animals upon which they rode; their cities, their buildings, and every particular; their mode of warfare; and also their religious worship. This he would do with as much ease, seemingly, as if he had spent his whole life among them"[65] (Italics added).

Based upon this information, it is proper to ask how Joseph was able to converse with his family so impressively about these ancient inhabitants. To help answer this question, we turn to the expressions of Elder John Taylor. In a letter to a clergyman in England concerning divine means of instruction, as used in teaching the Prophet, he wrote this brief statement: ". . . the Lord could teach a man more in five minutes than volumes would contain."[66] Likewise, the author has a friend who related that the Holy Ghost appeared to him on three separate occasions. After relating these sacred experiences, this friend declared: "I may not be a humble man, but I say that if the Holy Ghost were to teach me how to play the organ in five minutes, I would know how to play it better than anyone in the world!"

In presenting these comments, it is important to understand that an individual must be worthy and responsive to receiving this type of spiritual knowledge. The main role of the Holy Ghost is to testify of the Father and the Son, not to teach a person how to play an organ. My friend's comment was to emphasize how rapidly and thoroughly knowledge is conveyed through heavenly communications or visions.

Again, we obtain the following information from Lucy's history: "On the twenty-second of September,

1824, Joseph again visited the place where he found the plates the year previous; and supposing at this time that the only thing required, in order to possess [the plates] until the time for their translation, was to be able to keep the commandments of God—and he firmly believed he could keep every commandment which had been given him—he fully expected to carry [the plates] home with him.

"Therefore, having arrived at the place, and uncovering the plates, he put forth his hand and took them up, but, as he was taking them hence, the unhappy thought darted through his mind that probably there was something else in the box besides the plates, which would be of some [monetary] advantage to him. So, in the moment of excitement, he laid them down very carefully, for the purpose of covering the box, lest some one might happen to pass the way and get whatever there might be remaining in it. After covering it, he turned round to take the Record again, but behold it was gone, and where, he knew not, neither did he know the means by which it had been taken from him.

"At this, as a natural consequence, he was much alarmed. He kneeled down and asked the Lord why the Record had been taken from him; upon which the angel of the Lord [who was Moroni] appeared to him, and told him that he had not done as he had commanded, for in a former revelation he had been commanded not to lay the plates down, or put them for a moment out of his hands, until he got into the house and deposited them in a chest or trunk, having a good lock and key, and, contrary to this, he had laid them down with the view of securing some fancied or imaginary treasure that remained . . .

"Having some further conversation with the angel,

on this occasion, Joseph was permitted to raise the stone again, when he beheld the plates as he had done before. He immediately reached forth his hand to take them, but instead of getting them, as he anticipated, he was hurled back upon the ground with great violence. When he recovered, the angel was gone, and he arose and returned to the house, weeping for grief and disappointment."[67]

As has been previously written, Joseph was instructed by Moroni to tell his father of his visit and instructions. It was necessary that the Smith family remain together, not be pulled apart. To demonstrate this unity, Lucy Smith says that when her son was not able to take the plates in 1824, that "Joseph then related the circumstances in full, which gave us much uneasiness, as we were afraid that he might utterly fail in obtaining the Record through some neglect on his part. *We, therefore, doubled our diligence in prayer and supplication to God, in order that he might be more fully instructed in his duty . . .*"[68] (Italics added).

Lucy relates another incident that explains that the years between 1823 and 1827 were preparatory years for her son Joseph. A few months before the Prophet finally received the plates and instruments of revelation, his father sent him on an errand to the town of Manchester, not far from the Smith home. Expecting him around six o'clock in the evening, Joseph did not arrive home until late that evening. After entering the house, his father began questioning him as to why he was so late coming home. Joseph answered: "I have taken the severest chastisement that I have ever had in my life."

Questioning his son as to who had the right to find fault with him, the Prophet exclaimed, "Stop, father, stop, it was the angel of the Lord. As I passed by the hill of Cumorah, where the plates are, the angel met me and said that I had not been engaged enough in the work of the Lord; that the time had come for the record to be brought forth; and that I must be up and doing and set myself about the things which God had commanded me to do." Kindly, Joseph said, "But, father, give yourself no uneasiness concerning the reprimand which I have received, for I now know the course that I am to pursue, so all will be well."

Joseph's mother then added this comment: "It was also made known to him at this interview that he should make another effort to obtain the plates, on the twenty-second of the following September, but this he did not mention to us at that time."⁶⁹

From these narratives, we learn that Moroni was preparing Joseph to receive the plates and instruments of revelation that had been hidden away centuries earlier. This glorious event was to transpire on September 22, 1827. Now, approaching his twenty-second birthday, Joseph had the physical strength to defend his own person. Likewise, mentally and physically he was no longer a boy, but a man, who was capable and ready to do the important work that the Lord had called him to do.

"This four-year period from 1823 to 1827 was truly a condensed course of spiritual education for the Prophet as he matured in knowledge and stature. During these years, plus the two years following, records indicate that he had at least twenty-two separate interviews with Moroni . . ."⁷⁰

Truly, these were preparatory years for Joseph—spiritually, mentally, and physically. Therefore, this statement appropriately applies to the Prophet: "Preparation precedes power."

DESCRIPTION OF THE PROPHET JOSEPH

Various drawings of the Prophet Joseph, as an adult, depict him from being ordinary looking to strikingly handsome. Regarding his physical appearance, Elam Cheney, Sr. wrote the following description: "I belonged to the Nauvoo Legion, and Joseph was the General. Brother Joseph was a man weighing about two hundred pounds, fair complexion, and light brown hair. He was about six feet tall, sound bodied, very strong and quick— no breakage about his body. He most always wore a silk stock [scarf worn about the neck], and was smooth faced. He was very sympathetic and would talk to children and they liked him. He was honest, and was liked by everybody who knew him."[71]

With a similar description, Edwin F. Parry says: "Joseph Smith has been described as being six feet tall, weighing two hundred pounds, of light complexion with blue eyes and clear countenance. He was well built, athletic, [was] fond of manly sports. He had physical courage of the highest order."[72]

Lastly, President Joseph F. Smith, who was the nephew of the Prophet, wrote the following letter to a Brother Stanley Anderson in 1913. "You asked me the color of the eyes and the hair of the Prophet Joseph Smith. According to my best recollection, his eyes were blue with a slight grayish tinge, and they were large and full.

"His hair was a very light brown . . . ."[73]

As these commentaries have adequately described,

the Prophet Joseph was physically robust; therefore, he had the health and strength to perform the great work that the Lord had called him to do.

Paraphrasing from Joseph's History, he says that because his father's worldly circumstances were very limited, he and his immediate family were under the necessity of obtaining work, as opportunity afforded it, away from the family farm. Sometimes they worked near their home, other times they traveled farther away, and by so doing, the Smith family was able to maintain a comfortable living.

By way of a sad commentary, the Prophet says that in the year of 1823, his oldest brother, Alvin died. Then, in October, 1825, Joseph says that he hired with an older gentleman, Josiah Stoal, who lived in Chenango County, State of New York. This man had heard of a silver mine having been opened by the Spaniards in Harmony, Pennsylvania. Joseph further states that after working for this man for a month, he prevailed upon Mr. Stoal to cease digging after this treasure. "Hence arose the very prevalent story of my having been a money-digger."

As to how the Prophet met and married his wife Emma, he gives this explanation: During the time that he worked for Mr. Stoal, he boarded with a Mr. Issac Hale. It was while staying at this home, that Joseph met his daughter, Emma, and within a short time they mutually agreed to marry.

True to his word that he had seen the Father and the Son, he says, "Owing to my continuing to assert that I had seen a vision, persecution still followed me." Because of this persecution, Emma's family was very much opposed to the two being married. Without the approval of the Hale family, Joseph and Emma traveled to South Bainbridge, New York and were married January 18, 1827, at the house of Squire Tarbill. Without returning to the Hale home, Joseph and Emma moved in with Joseph's parents, and the Prophet farmed with his father that season (Joseph Smith—History 1:55-58).

FOURTH VISIT TO THE HILL CUMORAH

Nine months after he was married, Joseph made his fourth annual visit to the Hill Cumorah. However, this time he did not travel alone, but was accompanied by his wife, Emma, who patiently and faithfully waited at the base of the hill that evening. We wondered what they discussed together as they traveled toward Cumorah with a borrowed horse and buggy.[74]

As to what transpired on the momentous occasion, he says: "At length the time arrived for obtaining the plates, the Urim and Thummim, and the breastplate. On the twenty-second day of September, one thousand eight hundred and twenty-seven, having gone as usual at the end of another year to the place where they were deposited, the same messenger delivered them up to me with this charge: That I should be responsible for them; that if I should let them go carelessly, or through any neglect of mine, I should be cut off; but that if I would use all my endeavors to preserve them, until he, the messenger, should call for them, they should be protected" (Joseph Smith—History 1:59).

When morning arrived and breakfast was being served to family and friends, Lucy was concerned for the safety of her son and daughter-in-law. Finally, Joseph entered the house, but his mother did not see that her son had the plates. To calm his mother's concern, the

Prophet took her to another room and said: "Do not be uneasy, mother, all is right—see here, I have got a key."[75] Later in her writings, Lucy says that "which Joseph termed a key, was indeed, nothing more or less than the Urim and Thummim . . . ."[76]

Though we do not know the exact location where the plates were hidden, we may suppose that it was near the Hill Cumorah. As Lucy's history says: "The plates were secreted three miles from home [which is the same distance to the hill] in the following manner: Finding an old birch log much decayed, excepting the bark, which was in a measure sound, he took his pocket knife and cut the bark with some care, then turned it back and made a hole of sufficient size to receive the plates, and, laying them in the cavity thus formed, he replaced the bark; after which he laid across the log, in several places, some old stuff that happened to lay near, in order to conceal as much as possible the place in which they were deposited."[77]

After hearing of work, Joseph traveled the next day to Macedon to dig a well for a widow woman by the name of Wells. This labor provided money to pay a cabinet-maker for making a chest that would be used for storing the plates.

When the Prophet's father learned that several men were planning on finding the plates, he sent Emma to Macedon to tell Joseph. Again from Lucy, the following information is given: "Joseph kept the Urim and Thummim constantly about his person, by the use of which he could in a moment tell whether the plates were in any danger . . ." After Emma told her husband of what had transpired, the Prophet "looked in the Urim and Thummim and saw that the Record was as yet safe;

nevertheless, he concluded to return with his wife as something might take place that would render it necessary for him to be at home where he could take care of it."

Taking the plates from their hiding place, Joseph wrapped them in his linen frock [loose clothing] and placed them under his left arm and began his journey home.

Standing six feet tall and being physically robust, Joseph was able to defend himself from bodily harm. Though he was not planning on any trouble on his way home, he thought that it would be safer to leave the traveled road and go through the woods. In an attempt to jump over a fallen log, a man suddenly sprang up from behind it and gave Joseph a heavy blow with a gun. To most men, this type of punishment would have knocked them down. Still holding the plates that weighed fifty-pounds, Joseph turned around and knocked this man down with his fist and ran at top speed through the woods. About a half a mile farther, he was attacked again in the same manner as before. Again, he knocked this man down, as he did the first one, and continued running. Before Joseph reached home, he was assaulted a third time. In striking this last man, the Prophet dislocated his thumb, which, he did not notice until he came within sight of the house. From these encounters and running at top speed for three miles carrying heavy plates under one arm, the Prophet arrived home "speechless from fright and fatigue of running."[78]

Over the next several months while Joseph was in possession of the plates, many individuals tried to get them, even to the point of trespassing on the Smith property in search of them. So that they would not be found, Joseph moved them to different hiding places.

After safely bringing home the plates, Joseph commenced working with his father and brothers on the farm in order that he could be near the sacred record, which was entrusted to his care. One afternoon the Prophet came in from the field and put on his great coat [similar to a trench or rain coat] and left the house. When he returned home, he called for his mother to come down stairs. Soon, she came down and was shown a marvelous instrument to aid in the translation of the plates—"the breastplate spoken of in his history."[79]

CHAPTER EIGHT
INSTRUMENTS OF REVELATION

BREASTPLATE

When Moroni first told Joseph of the existence of the gold plates, he also said "that there were two stones in silver bows—and these stones, fastened to a *breastplate*, constituted what is called the Urim and Thummim— deposited with the plates; and the possession and use of these stones were what constituted 'seers' in ancient or former times; and that God had prepared them for the purpose of translating the book" (Joseph Smith—History 1:35) (Italics added).

Concerning the *breastplate* that held these two stones in silver bows, we recall from Lucy's history that after Joseph had put on his great coat and left the house, he soon returned and asked that his mother come down stairs. She says that when she came down to see what her son wanted, he handed her the *breastplate*. She then gives this informative description: "It was wrapped in a thin muslin [a sheer cotton fabric] handkerchief, so thin that I could feel its proportions without any difficulty.

"It was concave [rounded inward similar to the inside of a bowl] on one side and convex [rounded outward] on the other, and extended from the neck downwards, as far as the center of the stomach of a man of extraordinary size. It had four straps of the same material, for the purpose of fastening it to the breast, two of which ran back to go over the shoulders, and the other two were designed to fasten to the hips. They were just the width of two of my fingers (for I measured them), and they had holes in the end of them, to be convenient in fastening"[80] (Italics added). From Lucy's description, we have a better understanding how the breastplate looked and how it was worn by Joseph when he first began translating the *Book of Mormon*. Concluding her comments about the breastplate, the Prophet's mother says that after she "examined it, Joseph placed it in the *chest* with the Urim and Thummim"[81] (Italics added).

Unfortunately, the Prophet's mother does not describe what type of material the breastplate was made of, its thickness, or how much it weighed. If it were some type of metal, we may suppose that this material would be thin and light-weight so that the seer could wear this instrument comfortably while translating sacred records.

When Moroni first appeared to Joseph in 1823, this messenger told the boy-prophet that when he received the plates that he should not show them to any person; *"neither the breastplate* with the Urim and Thummim; *only to those to whom I should be commanded to show them*; if I did I should be destroyed" (Joseph Smith—History 1:42) (Italics added). Therefore, from what Lucy told about viewing the breastplate, it is proper to believe that Moroni had given Joseph permission to show them to his mother.

With interest, we read a description of this *chest* that had been made solely for the purpose of storing these instruments of revelation. In a published book about the life of the Prophet's brother Hyrum, it is written that this chest to hold the gold plates and Urim and Thummim is in the possession of Hyrum's descendants. "The name

'Alvin' is carved in the wood at the right of the metal lock set in wood an inch in width. Size—16" x 14 " x 6 " inside measurement. A sloping, inch thick wooden lid attached by two metal hinges to a 4" width strip across the top. A keyhole is located where the lock is. The chest contained also the *breastplate* and the Urim and Thummim"[82] (Italics added).

From the inside measurements of this chest, we find that the breast plate was less than sixteen inches in length and fourteen inches in width. Considering that the plates were stored in this box along with the breastplate and Urim and Thummim gives support to the supposition previously mentioned that the breastplate was thin and light-weight.

According to the *Book of Mormon* chronology, Moroni hid the records and the instruments of revelation in the Hill Cumorah around 421 A.D. When Joseph Smith was allowed to take these same sacred items, it was the year 1827. Therefore, when the Prophet showed the breastplate to his mother, this instrument to hold the Urim and Thummim was approximately 1,400 years old. Because of being tightly sealed in the box that was formed by laying stones together in some kind of cement and the power of God protecting it from corrosion and decay, the straps and the breastplate were in the same condition as when they had been deposited centuries earlier by this same Moroni (See Joseph Smith—History 1:52).

URIM AND THUMMIM

Our attention is now turned to the Urim and Thummim. From Joseph's history, we are informed that

Moroni told the boy-prophet there was a book deposited, written upon gold plates; also, that *there were two stones* in silver bows, and these stones, fastened to a breastplate, constituted what is called the Urim and Thummim (Joseph Smith—History 1:34-35).

These stones were not like a common rock that is found in and above the earth, but were clear and transparent. One account describes them as "two smooth *three-cornered diamonds set in glass* . . . connected with each other in much *the same way as old fashioned spectacles*"[83] (Italics added).

With a similar description, Elder Parley P. Pratt says: "With the records was found a curious instrument, called by the ancients the Urim and Thummim, which consisted of two transparent stones, *clear as crystal*, set in the two rims of a bow. It was an instrument by the use of which they received revelations of things distant, or of things past or future"[84] (Italics added).

Therefore, from these two references, we may properly suppose that these two stones were either fashioned from a diamond or a clear, quartz rock. However, with another understanding, Elder Orson Pratt has said: "You will perceive, Latter-day Saints, how this Urim and Thummim was formed in the first place. *It was not something that existed on the earth in a natural state, it was something made by the Lord.* He is a good mechanic; he understands how to make things."[85] No matter what they are made of, these stones were clear and transparent.

Concerning the Interpreters, Elder Bruce R. McConkie has written the following explanation: "A Urim and Thummim consists of two special stones called *seer stones* or *interpreters*. The Hebrew words *urim* and *thummim,* both plural, mean *lights and perfections.* Presumably one of the stones is called Urim and the other Thummim"[86] (Italics added).

With another understanding, Elder John Taylor expressed these thoughts: "I think the meaning of the name of this instrument is Light and Perfection, in other terms, communicating light perfectly, and intelligence perfectly, through a principle that God has ordained for that purpose."[87]

In the *Book of Mormon,* Ammon says: "The things are called *interpreters,* and no man can look in them except he be commanded, lest he should look for that he ought not and he should perish. And whosoever is commanded to look in them, the same is called *seer*" (Mosiah 8:13; 28:13-16) (Italics added).

As to which Urim and Thummim Joseph had, we are informed in a revelation to the three witnesses, that it was the same one that was used by the brother of Jared upon the mountain when he talked face to face with the premortal Lord (D&C 17:1; Ether 3:22-28).

From Lucy's history, it appears evident that Joseph was able to easily remove these instruments of revelation from their silver bows and replace them when he commenced translating. In support of this statement, we again read what the Prophet's mother said about the day that Joseph brought home the plates from the Hill Cumorah. Taking his mother in another room, the Prophet told her, "Do not be uneasy, mother, all is right—see here, I have got a key."

She said, "I knew not what he meant, but took the *article of which he spoke into my hands and examined it.* He took it again and left me, but said nothing respecting the Record." A few pages later in her history, she states: "That of which I spoke, which Joseph termed a key, was indeed, nothing more or less than the Urim and Thummim." Then, she gives this information:

"*Joseph kept the Urim and Thummim constantly about his person*, by the use of which *he could in a moment tell whether the plates were in any danger*"[88] (Italics added).

In support of this information, President Joseph F. Smith, the sixth President of the Church, has also written: "Joseph carried the Urim and Thummim with him, while the Plates and the Breast Plate were concealed to keep them from the mob, and by so doing was able to determine whether at any time they were in danger. The idea that the 'two stones,' commonly called the Urim and Thummim were 'set in the Breast Plate,' is entirely absurd, without doubt."[89]

From these statements, we are informed that the Prophet used these instruments of revelation *prior* to translating the *Book of Mormon*. Likewise, he was gifted in spiritual matters.

The reader is informed that from this point forward, this work will no longer follow the chronological events that transpired in the Prophet's life. The remaining chapters will focus on various aspects of his life that pertain to instruments of revelation, angelic visitations, and his calling to be a prophet of the Lord.

HOW JOSEPH TRANSLATED THE BOOK OF MORMON

As to how Joseph translated the *Book of Mormon*, we have no official explanation from him on how this actually happened, other than his statements that are recorded in the *Documentary History of the Church,* which say it was by the use of the Urim and Thummim.[90] Concerning part of the process that the Prophet had to do, we turn to a time during the translation of the *Book of Mormon* when Oliver Cowdery, who was Joseph's scribe, desired to be endowed with the gift of translation. In a revelation, Oliver obtained a promise from the Lord that he could translate a portion of the record. However, he was not successful in his attempt to do so. Greatly concerned why he was not able to translated, Joseph inquired of the Lord and received this revelation for Oliver: "Behold, you have not understood; you have supposed that I would give it unto you, when you took no thought save it was to ask me. But, behold, I say unto you, that you must *study it out in your mind; then you must ask me if it be right, and if it is right I will cause that your bosom shall burn within in you*; therefore, you *shall feel that it is right.*

"But if it be not right you shall have no such feelings, but you shall have a stupor of thought that shall cause you to forget the thing which is wrong . . . ."

The Lord then revealed this information: "Now, if you had known this you could have translated: nevertheless, it is not expedient that you should translate now" (D&C 9:7-9) (Italics added).

Though Joseph Smith, Jr. was highly gifted spiritually, he had to look at the characters on the plates by means of the Urim and Thummim and study it out in his mind; then, he had to ask the Lord if the interpretation was correct. If it was, he would *feel that it was right.*

In the next chapter, this work will present a more thorough study of a stone found by the Prophet Joseph called a Seer Stone. This singular stone is separate from the two stones called Urim and Thummim. With this information, we turn our attention to the following references.

One of the three witnesses to the *Book of Mormon*, David Whitmer, published a pamphlet in 1887, *Address to all Believers in Christ*. In it, he expresses his view as how the Prophet Joseph translated the plates. After describing how Joseph excluded the light from the instrument of revelation, he says: "In the darkness the spiritual light would shine. A piece of something resembling parchment would appear, and under it was the interpretation in English. Brother Joseph would read off the English to Oliver Cowdery, who was his principle scribe, and when it was written down and repeated to Brother Joseph to see if it was correct, then it would disappear, and another character with the interpretation would appear. Thus the *Book of Mormon* was translated by the gift and power of God and not by any power of man."[91]

Likewise, another witness to the *Book of Mormon*, Martin Harris, who served briefly as the Prophet's scribe, says: "By aid of the Seer Stone, [Urim and Thummim] sentences would appear and were read by the Prophet and written by Martin, and when finished he would say 'written;' and if correctly written, the sentence would disappear and another appear in its place; but if not written correctly it remained until corrected, so that the translation was just as it was engraven on the plates, precisely in the language then used."[92]

Though these statements are highly interesting to read, it is important to point out that neither the Prophet Joseph Smith, nor his main scribe, Oliver Cowdery, substantiate these claims.

Concerning the means to translate the plates, Oliver says: "These were days never to be forgotten—to sit under the sound of a voice dictated by the inspiration of heaven, awakened the utmost gratitude of this bosom! Day after day I continued, uninterrupted, to write from his mouth, as he [the Prophet Joseph Smith], *translated with the Urim and Thummim*, or as the Nephites would have said, *'Interpreters,'* the history or record called *"The Book of Mormon"*[93] (Italics added).

Though Joseph used the Interpreters, Elder B. H. Roberts says it "was not merely a mechanical process. It required the utmost concentration of mental and spiritual force possessed by the Prophet, in order to exercise the gift of translation through the means of the sacred instruments provided for that work."[94]

From using this instrument of revelation, the *Urim and Thummim*, and by mental and spiritual concentration, Joseph Smith, Jr. was able to accomplish the marvelous work of translating the *Book of Mormon*. Therefore, he is appropriately called the Prophet and Seer of the latter-days.

CHAPTER NINE
THE PROPHET'S SEER STONE

Because there are published statements which say that the Prophet Joseph sometimes used the Urim and Thummim and other times a Seer Stone in the work of translating the *Book of Mormon*, let us find out more about this *Seer Stone*.

During the time that Joseph received the gold plates and the Urim and Thummim, there were various people who were classified as being psychic or clairvoyant, either through telepathy or thought transference. Likewise, certain individuals resorted to crystal-gazing or seeking information through peep-stones.[95]

Through inspiration, Joseph was prompted to move the plates to different hiding places so that they would not be taken from him before they were translated. On one occasion, the Prophet hid them in a cooper's shop (where they made or repaired wooden casks or tubs) and hid them in flax which was stored in the loft of the shop. When night came, several men ransacked the place, but left after not finding the plates.

"In a few days afterwards," says Lucy Smith, "we learned the cause of this last move [by these men]—why their curiosity led them in the direction of the cooper's shop. A young woman by the name of Chase, sister to Willard Chase, found *a green glass through which she could see many very wonderful things*, and among her great discoveries she said that *she saw the precise place where 'Joe Smith kept his gold Bible hid,'* and obedient to her directions, the mob gathered their forces and laid siege to the cooper's shop.

"Notwithstanding their disappointment in not finding the plates in the shop, their confidence was not in the least shaken in Miss Chase, for they still went from place to place by her direction, determined to get, if possible, the much desired object of their search"[96] (Italics added).

Some time prior to the time that the Prophet began translating the *Book of Mormon* in 1829, he obtained a Seer Stone. In describing how it looked, we again turn to Elder B. H. Roberts for information: "The 'Seer Stone' referred to here was *a chocolate colored, somewhat egg-shaped stone* which the prophet found while digging a well in company with his brother Hyrum. *It possessed some of the qualities of a Urim and Thummim . . .*"[97] (Italics added).

Though the following information cannot be verified, yet this information supports, in part, what Elder Roberts wrote that a Seer Stone possesses some of the qualities of a Urim and Thummim. In a journal by Priddy Meeks in 1879, he wrote the following: "Seer Stones, or peep-stones as they are more commonly called, were very plenty [plentiful] about Parowan [Utah]. I rather being a gifted person in knowing a peep-stone when seeing one, altho [sic] I have never found one yet that I could see in, *a seer-stone appears to me to be the connecting link between the visible and invisible world . . .*

"*It is not safe to depend on peep-stones* in any case where evil spirits have the power to put false appearances before them while looking in a peep-stone. If evil influences will not interfere, the verdict will be as true as preaching. That is my experience in the matter. Also, the Patriarch, Hyrum Smith, the brother of the Prophet Joseph Smith, held the same idea, but stated that our faith was not strong enough to overcome the evil influences that might interfere . . . I have seen peep-stones as well polished as a fiddle, with a nice hole thro [sic] one end that belonged to the Ancients [the Nephites]. I asked Bro. Smith the use for that hole. He said the same as for a watch chain, to keep from losing it. *He said in time of war the Nephites had the advantage of their enemies, by looking in the seer stone, which would reveal whatever they wished to know*"[98] (Italics added).

As we notice, Brother Meeks interchangeably uses the words peepstone and seer stone. In addition, he says that it is not safe to depend on them for correct information because evil spirits have power to put false appearances before those who look in a peep-stone.

Such was the case with Hiram Page, who was a member of the Church. He had a certain peep-stone and professed to be receiving revelations by it concerning the order of the Church. Several members had been deceived by these claims, and even Oliver Cowdery was wrongly influenced by them. The Prophet inquired of the Lord concerning this matter, and a revelation dated September, 1830 was directed to Oliver Cowdery that no one was appointed to receive commandments and revelations for the Church excepting Joseph Smith, Jr. The revelation also directed Oliver to take Hiram Page by himself and talk to him upon the subject. He was instructed to tell him that which he had received through that stone was not of the Lord and that Satan deceived him (D&C 28).

Returning to the Prophet's Seer Stone, Brigham Young says that on December 27, 1841, "I met with the Twelve at Brother Joseph's [home]. He conversed with us in a familiar manner on a variety of subjects, and explained to us the Urim and Thummim which he found with the plates, called in the Book of Mormon the Interpreters. *He said that every man who lived on the earth was entitled to a seer stone,* and should have one, but they are kept from them in consequences of their wickedness, and most of those who do find one make an evil use of it. *He showed us his seer stone*"[99] (Italics added).

With a different understanding of what happened at that same meeting, we read: "On Christmas day of 1841, Elder [Wilford] Woodruff says that he and other members of the Twelve visited the home of Hyrum Kimball, who, before they left, presented each of the Twelve with a lot to which he gave them the deed. On the 26th and 27th, the Twelve visited the home of the Prophet, and on one of these days Elder Woodruff says in his journal *that the Prophet showed him and others for the first time the Urim and Thummim*[100] (Italics added).

In speaking of obtaining the plates, the Urim and Thummim, and the Breastplate on September 22, 1827, the Prophet says, "By the wisdom of God, they remained safe in my hands, until I had accomplished by them what was required at my hand. When, according to arrangements, the messenger called for *them*, I delivered *them up to him* [which date the Prophet never gave]; *and he has them in his charge* until this day, being the second day of May, one thousand eight hundred and thirty-eight."[101] With this information, we know that in

December 1841, the Twelve were not shown the Urim and Thummim, but the Prophet's Seer Stone.

Elder B. H. Roberts then writes this short commentary: "On one occasion [Martin] Harris sought to test the genuineness of the prophet's procedure in the matter of translation, as follows:

"'Martin said that after continued translation they would become weary and would go down to the river and exercise in throwing stones out on the river, etc. While so doing on one occasion, *Martin found a stone very much resembling the one used for translating,* and on resuming their labors of translation, Martin put in place [of the Seer Stone] the stone that he had found. He said that the prophet remained silent unusually and intently gazing in darkness, no trace of the usual sentence appearing. Much surprised, Joseph exclaimed: 'Martin! What is the matter? All is dark as Egypt.' Martin's countenance betrayed him, and the prophet asked Martin why he had done so. Martin said, to stop the mouths of fools, who had told him that the prophet had learned those sentences and was merely repeating them'"[102] (Italics added).

POSSIBLE REASONS FOR JOSEPH SMITH'S SEER STONE

Regarding possible reasons for the Prophet's Seer Stone, Brother Andrew Jenson, who was the Church Historian for several years, wrote the following information about Martin Harris: "On Sunday, September 4, 1870, Martin Harris addressed a congregation of the Saints in Salt Lake City. He related an incident which occurred during the time that he wrote that portion of the translation of the *Book of Mormon* which he was favored to write direct from the mouth of the Prophet Joseph Smith, and said that the Prophet *possessed a Seer Stone, by which he was enabled to translate as well as from the Urim and Thummim, and for convenience he then used the Seer Stone*"[104] (Italics added).

As was written in the previous chapter, David Whitmer expressed a similar description as did Martin Harris. By placing the Seer Stone in a hat, the Prophet would cover his face with the hat, excluding all light, and a piece of parchment would appear and under it was the interpretation in English. If written correctly, another character with the interpretation would appear, thereby, the *Book of Mormon* was translated by the gift and power of God and not by any power of man.[105]

From these statements by two of the three witnesses to the *Book of Mormon*, we get the impression that Joseph used both instruments in the process of translating the gold plates. However, according to Oliver Cowdery and the Prophet Joseph Smith it was by the Urim and Thummim.

After presenting what Martin Harris and David Whitmer expressed, Elder B. H. Roberts wrote the following summation: "There remains, however the statements of Whitmer and Harris . . . And, by the way, in passing, I want to ask those who stand up so stoutly for the vindication of what Messrs Whitmer and Harris have chanced to say on the subject of translation—what about the Lord's description of the same thing in the *Doctrine and Covenants*? Are they not interested in vindicating that description? I care very little, comparatively, for what Messers Whitmer and Harris have said about the subject. I care *everything for what the Lord has to say about it* . . .

"They say [Harris and Whitmer] the interpretations appeared in English, under the Nephite characters in Urim and Thummim [Note: he does not write Seer Stone]; we say, if so, then that interpretation, after being wrought out in the Prophet's mind, was reflected into Urim and Thummim and held visible there until written. The English interpretation was a reflex from the Prophet's mind . . .

"It is asked, however, 'Shall we understand that Urim and Thummim are not what they have hitherto purported to be?' . . . if by 'purported to be' is meant that the Urim and Thummim did the mental work of trans-lating—that the instrument did everything, and the Prophet nothing except to read off what the instrument interpreted—*then the sooner that theory is abandoned the better*; there is nothing in the word of God, or right reason, to warrant it . . ."[106] (Italics added).

Returning to what has been written in the previous chapter, Elder Roberts says, "I repeat, then, that the translation of the Book of Mormon . . . was not merely a mechanical process, but required the utmost concentra-tion of mental and spiritual force possessed by the prophet, in order to exercise the gift of translation through the means of the sacred instruments provided for the work."[107]

With this information, we continue our study of the Prophet's Seer Stone. Elder Orson F. Whitney provides the following: "David Whitmer, one of the Three Witnesses to the Book of Mormon . . . found fault with the Prophet for receiving revelations *without the aid of a Seer-Stone*, previously used by him, but laid aside after he had fully mastered his gift. David seems to have regarded the gift of revelation in the Prophet as of less consequence than the stone, *which was no longer needed*"[108] (Italics added).

Likewise, Elder Orson Pratt "declared at such times Joseph used the 'seer stone' when inquiring of the Lord, and receiving revelations, but that he was so *thoroughly endowed with the inspiration of the Almighty and the spirit of revelation that he often received them without any instrument or other means than the operation of the Spirit upon his mind*"[109] (Italics added).

From these statements by Elders Whitney and Pratt, it gives the impression that the Prophet Joseph only used the Seer Stone in the beginning of his ministry as a means of receiving information from the Lord. Though these remarks are interesting to read, they have not been substantiated by what the Prophet has written or spoken. If they are true, then *perhaps* his Seer Stone *was a physical means of increasing his faith* during the early stages of his ministry to receiving revelations and information from the Lord?

WHERE IS JOSEPH'S SEER STONE?

Because the Prophet no longer needed the Seer Stone, it is reasonable to ask what he did with it. To answer this question, we turn to David Whitmer, one of the three witnesses: "After the translation of the *Book of Mormon* was finished, early in the spring of 1830, before April 6th, *Joseph gave the stone to Oliver Cowdery*, and told me, as well as the rest [of those present], that he was through with it, *and he did not use the stone any more.* He said he *was through the work that God had given him the gift to perform*, except to preach the gospel. He told us that we would all have to depend on the Holy Ghost hereafter, to be guided into truth and obtain the will of the Lord. The revelations *after this* came through Joseph as 'mouthpiece;' that is, he would enquire of the Lord, pray and ask concerning a matter, *and speak out the revelation . . .*"[110] (Italics added).

This knowledge of Joseph giving the Seer Stone to Oliver Cowdery was not known to the author when writing his first book, *Mysteries of the Kingdom*. On page 102, I unknowingly wrote the following statement: "It is noteworthy that when Oliver Cowdery was excommunicated from the Church, he took the Prophet's seer stone; then gave it to President Brigham Young when he rejoined the Church."

So where is Joseph's Seer Stone? The following information provides the answer. When the Manti, Utah temple was dedicated, it has been stated that the Urim and Thummim was on the altar. From President Wilford Woodruff, we read his informative words concerning this private dedicatory service in this holy edifice: "Before leaving, I consecrated upon the altar *the Seer Stone that Joseph Smith found by revelation* some thirty feet under the earth (ground), and carried by him through life"[111] (Italics added).

Returning to the statement that the Prophet gave his Seer Stone to Oliver Cowdery, we learn from a personal letter written by President Joseph F. Smith, a Counselor in the First Presidency at the time, how the Church obtained this instrument: "The little stone you refer to is in the *care or possession of President John Taylor*. He having received it after the death of Pres. B. Young, who had it in his possession, *he having received it from*

Oliver Cowdery after he rejoined the Church"[112] (Italics added). Elder B. H. Roberts writes that in speaking with President Joseph F. Smith that the Church was in possession of the Prophet Joseph's Seer Stone.[113]

Concerning the Seer Stone and Urim and Thummim, Elder Joseph Fielding Smith, who is classified as one of the great scholars of the Church, and who became the tenth President of the Church, says: "We have been taught since the days of the Prophet that *the Urim and Thummim were returned with the plates to the angel.* We have not record of the Prophet having the Urim and Thummim after the organization of the Church. Statements of translations by the Urim and Thummim after that date are evidently errors. The statement has been made that the Urim and Thummim was on the altar in the Manti Temple when that building was dedicated. The Urim and Thummim so spoken of, however, *was The Seer Stone which was in the possession of the Prophet Joseph Smith in early days. This Seer Stone is now in the possession of the Church.*

"While the statements has been made by some writers that the Prophet Joseph Smith used a *seer stone* part of the time in his translating of the record, *and information points to the fact that he did have in his possession such a stone, yet there is no authentic statement in the history of the Church which states that the use of such a stone was made in that translation.* The information is all *hearsay,* and personally, I do not believe that this stone was used for that purpose. The reason I give for this conclusion is found in the statement of the Lord to the Brother of Jared as recorded in Ether 3:22-24.

"These stones, the Urim and Thummim which were given to the Brother of Jared, were preserved for this *very purpose of translating the record*, both of the Jaredites and the Nephites. Then again the Prophet was impressed by Moroni with the fact that these stones were given for that very purpose. It hardly seems reasonable to suppose that the Prophet would substitute something evidently inferior under these circumstances. *It may have been so, but it is so easy for a story of this kind to be circulated due to the fact that the Prophet did possess a seer stone, which he may have used for some other purposes*"[114] (Italics added).

As has been written in this chapter, we know that the Prophet Joseph Smith had a Seer Stone, but for what reason, we are not fully informed. We know that the Church is in possession of it, but beyond this information, we are left to wonder about its purpose and function.

CHAPTER TEN
ITEMS VIEWED BY
THE THREE WITNESSES

LAW OF WITNESSES

During the translation of certain passages in the *Book of Mormon*, the Prophet Joseph Smith and his scribe, Oliver Cowdery, learned that three special witnesses would be designated to "testify to the truth of the book and the things therein" (2 Ne. 27:12, 11:3, and Ether 5:2-4).

Paraphrasing what has been written by Elder Joseph Fielding Smith, he says that Joseph Smith was alone when he had the First Vision, alone when Moroni appeared to him, and alone when he received the plates. However, after that he was not alone. The Lord called other witnesses to testify and support his testimony.[115]

"Whenever the Lord has established a dispensation by revealing his gospel and by conferring priesthood and keys upon men," Elder Bruce R. McConkie says, "he has acted in accordance with the *law of witnesses* which he himself ordained. This law is: 'In the mouth of two or three witnesses shall every word be established' (2 Cor. 13:1; Deut. 17:6; 19:15; Matt. 18:15-16; John 8:12-29) (Italics added).

"Never does one man stand alone in establishing a new dispensation of revealed truth, or in carrying the burden of such a message and warning to the world.

In every dispensation, from Adam to the present, two or more witnesses have always joined their testimonies, thus leaving their hearers without excuse in the Day of Judgment should the testimony be rejected"[116] (Italics added).

Regarding these three special witnesses who were mentioned in the *Book of Mormon* passages, it seems a logical choice that two scribes to the Prophet, Martin Harris and Oliver Cowdery, and a friend, David Whitmer, who requested that Joseph Smith, his wife Emma, and Oliver come and stay at his parent's home to translate the plates, would *desire* to become these witnesses. These three men were most prominent in assisting to bring forth this great work.

Concerning their individual and collective *desire*, the Prophet says, "Almost immediately after we [Joseph and Oliver] had made this discovery [of these translated passages] it occurred to Oliver Cowdery, David Whitmer and . . . Martin Harris . . . that they would have me inquire of the Lord to know if they might not obtain of him the privilege to be these three special witnesses; and finally *they became so very solicitous, and urged me so much to inquire* that at length I complied; and *through the Urim and Thummim* [Note: Not the Seer Stone], I obtained of the Lord for them the following: Revelation to Oliver Cowdery, David Whitmer, and Martin Harris, at Fayette, Seneca County, New York, June 1829, given previous to their viewing the plates concerning the Book of Mormon"[117] (Italics added).

In this revelation, which is designated as Section 17 in the *Doctrine and Covenants*, the Lord told these three men that by their "faith," they shall have a "view of the *plates*, and also the *breastplate*, the *sword of Laban*, the *Urim and Thummim* . . . and the *miraculous directors* . . ." (Italics added). Therefore, these special witnesses would actually see five sacred items that are spoken of in the *Book of Mormon*. This truly was a glorious promise.

According to Lucy Smith, she says that as soon as the *Book of Mormon* was translated—[which was between April 7, 1829, and the first part of June of that same year][118]—the Prophet sent a messenger to his parents requesting that they come to the Whitmer home in Waterloo; which was located about twenty-five miles from Palmyra, in a neighborhood called Fayette, Seneca County, New York.[119]

"That same evening," Lucy says, "we conveyed this intelligence to Martin Harris, for we loved the man, although his weakness had cost us much trouble. Hearing this [news that the *Book of Mormon* was translated], he greatly rejoiced, and determined to go straightway to Waterloo to congratulate Joseph upon his success. Accordingly, the next morning, we all set off together, and before sunset met Joseph and Oliver at Mr. Whitmer's [home]."

Following their usual morning services of reading, singing, and praying, "Joseph arose from his knees, and approaching Martin Harris with a solemnity that thrills through my veins to this day, when it occurs to my recollection, said, 'Martin Harris, you have got to humble yourself before God this day, that you may obtain a forgiveness of your sins. If you do, it is the will of God that you should look upon the plates, in company with Oliver Cowdery and David Whitmer.'"[120] Therefore, according to prophecy as stated in the mentioned passages from the *Book of Mormon*, it was not by chance that Oliver Cowdery, David Whitmer, and Martin Harris were all at the Whitmer home that memorable day.

In the Prophet's history, he writes: "Not many days after the above commandment was given, we four . . . Martin Harris, David Whitmer, Oliver Cowdery and myself, agreed to retire into the woods, and try to obtain, by fervent and humble prayer, the fulfillment of the promises given in the above revelation—*that they should have a view of the plates*"[121] (Italics added).

In this grove of trees not far from the Whitmer home, they all knelt down. By agreement, Joseph first offered a vocal prayer to our Heavenly Father. Then, in succession, each of his friends did likewise. Following their first attempt of praying, no manifestation of divine favor was granted. They again observed the same order of prayer, but did not receive the desired blessing.

Feeling it was because of his transgressions that no answer was received, Martin Harris proposed that he withdraw from the group. After Martin withdrew, the three knelt in prayer. Within minutes, they beheld a light of exceeding brightness, and behold, an angel stood before them. The Prophet says: "In his hands he held the plates which we had been praying for these to have a view of. He turned over the leaves one by one, so that we could see them, and discern the engravings thereon distinctly . . . ."[122]

After four years of visiting the Hill Cumorah, Joseph was allowed to take the plates home. He moved them to different hiding places, prior to them being translated. He alone was allowed to see and touch and translate these sacred records. Even on this special day when these witnesses were allowed to view the plates, Moroni held them and turned the pages. Not one of these privileged men was allowed to hold them. These plates were reserved solely for the head of the final dispensation to hold and translate them—even the Prophet Joseph Smith. Truly he alone was foreordained to accomplish this great work that God had called him to do (See Joseph Smith—History 1:33-42).

This same angel then turned to David Whitmer and said: "David blessed is the Lord, and he that keeps his commandments." Immediately after this, they heard a voice in the bright light which shown above them, saying: "These plates have been revealed by the power of God, and they have been translated by the power of God. The translation of them which you have seen is correct, and I command you to bear record of what you now see and hear."[123]

Joseph Smith now left David and Oliver and went in search of Martin Harris. He found him at a considerable distance fervently engaged in prayer. Hearing Joseph approach, he opened his eyes and said that he had not yet prevailed with the Lord, and he earnestly pleaded with the Prophet to join him that he, too, might be blessed to see a vision of the plates.

Joseph agreed, and before they had prayed very long the same vision was open to their view and they beheld the same messenger. The angel again turned the leaves one by one, and the voice was heard speaking the same words. Overjoyed, Martin exclaimed, "Tis enough; tis enough; mine eyes have beheld; mine eyes have beheld; and jumping up, he shouted, 'Hosanna,' blessing God."[124]

Though the following information is not written in the Prophet's history, David Whitmer, in a conversation with Elders Orson Pratt and Joseph F. Smith, on September 7, 1878, declared, in part: "Joseph, Oliver, and I were together when I saw them [the plates]. We not only saw the *plates of the Book of Mormon*, but also *the brass plates, the plates of the Book of Ether* . . . and *many other plates* . . . there appeared, as it were, *a table with many records*, or plates upon it, besides the plates of the Book of Mormon, also the *sword of Laban*, the *directors* [the ball which Lehi had called Liahona], and the *Interpreters*. I saw them just as plainly as I see this bed (striking the bed beside him with his hand), *and I heard the voice of the Lord*, as distinctly as I ever heard anything in my life, declaring that the records of the plates of the *Book of Mormon* were translated by the gift and power of God"[125] (Italics added).

DESCRIPTION AND WEIGHT
OF THE PLATES

Concerning the plates that the witnesses saw, the Prophet gives the following description in *The Wentworth Letter*: "These records were engraven on plates which had the *appearance of gold*; each plate was *six inches wide and eight inches long*, and not so thick as common tin. They were *filled with engravings*, in *Egyptian characters*, and *bound together in a volume as the leaves of a book, with three rings running through the whole*. The volume was something six inches in thickness, a part of which was sealed. The characters on the unsealed part were small, and beautifully engraved. The whole book exhibited many marks of antiquity in its construction, and much skill in the art of engraving . . ."[126] (Italics added).

Regarding the Egyptian characters engraved on the plates, we turn to the writings of Nephi, who was the son of Lehi, and read his words: "Yea, I make a record in the language of my father, which consists of the learning of the Jews and the *language of the Egyptians*" (1 Nephi 1:2) (Italics added). From this, we learn that from the time of the first Nephi spoken of in the *Book of Mormon* until Moroni deposited them in the Hill Cumorah, each of the record-keepers used the language of the Egyptians.

Adding to the description given by the Prophet concerning the plates, Elder Orson Pratt in a discourse given in the Salt Lake City Tabernacle, on January 2, 1859, says: "Upon each side of the leaves of these plates there were fine engravings, *which were stained with a black, hard stain, so as to make the letters more legible and easier to read.* Through the back of the plates were three rings, which held them together, and *through which a rod might easily be passed, serving as a greater convenience for carrying them*; the construction and form of the plates being similar to the gold, brass, and lead plates of the ancient Jews in Palestine"[127] (Italics added). Since there are no quotations from the Prophet in this description, we may assume that Elder Pratt received his information from the teachings of the Prophet rather than from his writings.

Pertaining to the weight of the plates, the Prophet's brother, William Smith, said that he never did see them uncovered, "but I handled them and hefted them while wrapped in a tow frock *and judged them to have weighed about sixty pounds . . .*"[128] (Italics added).

B. F. Cummings, who was the editor of the *Liahona, The Elders' Journal*, published the following information, on July 18, 1908: "Joseph Smith the Prophet was a man of splendid physique and great physical strength, and it was no trick at all for him to walk miles [after leaving with them from the Hill Cumorah] with a weight of *50 or even 65 pounds* under his arm . . ."[129] (Italics added). Though we have no official statement concerning the weight of the plates from these published statements, we may suppose that they weighed between 50 and 60 pounds.

DESCRIPTION OF THE BREASTPLATE

As has been written in Chapter Eight of this work, the breastplate was concave on one side and convex on the other, and extended less than sixteen inches from the neck downward, and was less than fourteen inches in width. It had four straps of the same material, for the purpose of fastening it to the breast of the translator, two of which ran back to go over the shoulders, and the other two were designed to fasten to the hips. We have no knowledge of the material the breastplate was made of. If it were some type of metal, we may suppose that this material would be thin and lightweight so that the seer could wear this instrument comfortably while translating sacred records.

DESCRIPTION AND PURPOSE OF THE URIM AND THUMMIM

The Prophet describes the Urim and Thummim as "two stones in silver bows . . ." (Joseph Smith—History 1:35). One account describes them as "two smooth three-cornered diamonds set in glass . . . connected with each other in much the same way as old fashioned spectacles."

Elder Parley P. Pratt says they "consisted of two transparent stones, clear as crystal, set in the two rims of a bow." We are not informed of the material the Urim and Thummim are made of. Through these instruments of revelation, the Prophet Joseph Smith was able to translate the *Book of Mormon*, and receive information and revelations from the Lord.

DESCRIPTION OF THE SWORD OF LABAN

The only description we have of the sword of Laban is from the first Nephi spoken of in the *Book of Mormon*. After Nephi found Laban on the ground, drunken with wine, he says, "I beheld his sword, and I drew it forth from the sheath thereof; and the hilt thereof was of pure gold, and the workmanship thereof was exceedingly fine, and I saw that the blade thereof was of the most precious steel" (1 Nephi 4:9).

DESCRIPTION AND PURPOSE
OF THE MIRACULOUS DIRECTORS

The only description we have of the miraculous directors is from the first Nephi spoken of in the Book of Mormon. "And it came to pass that as my father [Lehi] arose in the morning, and went forth to the tent door, to his great astonishment he beheld upon the ground a round ball of curios workmanship, and it was of fine brass. And within the ball were two spindles; and the one pointed the way wither we should go into the wilderness." He then tells how the spindles operated: "And it came to pass that I, Nephi, beheld the pointers which were in the ball, that they did work according to the faith and diligence and heed which we did give unto them. And there was also written upon them a new writing, which was plain to be read, which did give us understanding concerning the ways of the Lord; and it was written and changed from time to time, according to the faith and diligence which he gave unto it . . ." (1 Nephi 16:10, 28-29).

In the Book of Mormon, this instrument is usually referred to as "the ball." It is sometimes called a "compass" or "director." The word "Liahona" is only used once in the Book of Mormon. In charging his son, Helaman, to take care of the records, Alma the younger said: "And now, my son, I have somewhat to say concerning the thing which our fathers call a ball, or director—or our fathers called it Liahona, which is, being interpreted, a compass; and the Lord prepared it" (Alma 37:38) (Italics added).

By this instrument of revelation, food was found, directions of travel were given, and messages were written upon the spindles. According to Alma the younger, "For just as surely as this director did bring our fathers, by following its course, to the Promised Land, shall the words of Christ, if we follow their course, carry us beyond this vale of sorrow into a far better land of promise" (See Alma 37:38-45).

THE JOY OF THE PROPHET
AND WITNESSES

By their faith, the Prophet Joseph Smith and the three witnesses, Oliver Cowdery, David Whitmer, and Martin Harris, were able to see these sacred items on that memorable day in June of 1829. The following information is from Lucy Smith: "When they returned to the house it was between three and four o'clock p. m. Mrs. Whitmer, Mr. Smith [Joseph Smith, Sr.] and myself, were sitting in a bedroom at the time. On coming in, Joseph threw himself down beside me [on the bed], and exclaimed, 'Father, mother, you do not know how happy I am: *the Lord has now caused the plates to be shown to three besides myself.* They have seen an angel, who has testified to them, and they will have to bear witness to the truth of what I have said, for now they know for themselves, that I do not go about to deceive the people, and I feel as if I was relieved of a burden which was almost too heavy for me to bear, and it rejoices my soul, that I am not any longer to be entirely alone in the world.' Upon this, Martin Harris came in: he seemed almost overcome with joy, and testified boldly to what he had both seen and heard. And so did David and Oliver, adding that no tongue could express the joy in their hearts, and the greatness of the things which they had both seen and heard"[130] (Italics added).

In accordance with the revelation they received and by direct commandment from the voice of the Lord when they viewed the plates, the three witnesses gave to the world their united testimony in writing, which was at the end of the first edition, and following the title page of all subsequent editions. Their testimony, together with the testimony of eight other witnesses who also beheld the plates, has been published in every copy of the *Book of Mormon* since it was published (The reader is encouraged to read their combined testimony).

THE WITNESSES NEVER DENIED
THEIR TESTIMONIES

From documented statements, we know that the three witnesses of the *Book of Mormon* were true and faithful to their testimony throughout their lives. "The time came," says, Elder Joseph Fielding Smith, "when all three of the special witnesses became estranged from Joseph Smith and departed from the Church because of their spirit of rebellion against the Prophet and the work. Oliver Cowdery and David Whitmer were dealt with for their fellowship and excommunication from the Church. Martin Harris simply drifted away without any action being taken against him in any official way. While the Prophet lived, they retained their bitterness of spirit and remained aloof, but during all those years, and to the end of life, all three were steadfast in their testimony as found in the *Book of Mormon*. In the year 1848 after the Church had been driven from Nauvoo, Oliver Cowdery returned to the Church at Kanesville [Iowa, which later was named Council Bluff] and humbly begged to be readmitted as a member. Martin Harris also sought again a place and standing in the Church, and in the year 1870 he came to Utah to make his home. He died in 1875, at Clarkston, Utah, at the age of 92 years. David Whitmer never came back to the Church, but shortly before his death, in refutation of the statements that had gone forth that he had denied his testimony, he published it again to the world . . . ."[131] (Italics added)

CONCLUSION

From what has been presented in this chapter, we know by their faith that Oliver Cowdery, David Whitmer, and Martin Harris, along with the Prophet Joseph Smith, saw the plates, breastplate, sword of Laban, Urim and Thummim, and the miraculous directors, as promised by the Lord. Though these special witnesses became estranged from the Prophet and left the Church, they never denied their testimony of what they had seen and heard. Thankfully, Oliver Cowdery and Martin Harris returned as members of the Church. We conclude our study of the Three Witnesses by quoting a small portion of their combined testimony: "And we declare with words of soberness, that an angel of God came down from heaven, and he brought and laid before our eyes, that we beheld and saw the plates, and the engravings thereon; and we know that it is by the grace of God the Father, and our Lord Jesus Christ, that we beheld and bear record that these things are true."

CHAPTER ELEVEN
ANGELS APPEAR AND RESTORE PRIESTHOOD AND KEYS

"ALL PRIESTHOOD IS MELCHIZEDEK"

Members of the Church believe and teach that there is only one true gospel, only one true Church, and we have the only true Priesthood. Concerning Priesthood, the Prophet Joseph Smith says: "*All priesthood is Melchizedek, but there are different portions or degrees of it*"[132] (Italics added).

In Section 107 of the *Doctrine and Covenants*, titled a revelation on the Priesthood, the Lord revealed through the Prophet that in the Church *there are two priesthoods, namely, the Melchizedek and Aaronic, including the Levitical Priesthood.* Regarding the Melchizedek Priesthood, it is written: "All other authorities or offices in the Church are appendages to this priesthood." This means that all offices and officers, all organizations and programs, and all members of the Church are subject to the Melchizedek Priesthood. All things in the Church are appendages to the priesthood; thus, the Melchizedek Priesthood is the governing power that allows individuals, based upon faithfulness, to gain eternal life.

With more clarification, President Joseph F. Smith, the sixth President of the Church, said in a General Conference: ". . . all blessings, all offices, all callings, and all authority in this Church come under and are embraced in the holy Melchizedek Priesthood, which is after the order of the Son of God. *There is no office growing out of this Priesthood that is or can be greater than the Priesthood itself.* It is from the Priesthood that the office derives its authority and power. *No office gives authority to the Priesthood. No office adds to the power of the Priesthood.* But all offices in the Church derive their power, their virtue, their authority, from the Priesthood . . . No office of an Apostle, no office of a President, no office of a High Priest, or a Seventy, or an Elder, *is greater than the Melchizedek Priesthood.* I hope you will understand that. If an apostle has any authority at all, he derives it from the Melchizedek Priesthood, which is after God's order, and he cannot have it any other way. There is no authority except it comes from that Priesthood . . . Out of the Melchizedek Priesthood grows the Lesser Priesthood, which is called the Priesthood after the order of Aaron. This is an appendage to the Melchizedek Priesthood. The office of an Elder, of a High Priest, of a Seventy—all the offices in the Church are simply appendages to the Melchizedek Priesthood, *and grow out of it*"[133] (Italics added).

Returning to Section 107 we read: "But there are two divisions or grand heads—one is the Melchizedek Priesthood, and the other is the Aaronic or Levitical Priesthood." Concerning these, the Prophet says: "Although there are two Priesthoods, yet the Melchizedek Priesthood comprehends the Aaronic or Levitical Priesthood, and is the grand head, and holds the highest authority which pertains to the Priesthood, and the keys of the Kingdom of God in all ages of the world to the latest posterity on the earth, and is the channel through which all knowledge, doctrine, the plan of salvation, and every important matter is revealed from heaven."[134] With this understanding, we now turn our attention to events that led to the Prophet Joseph Smith and Oliver Cowdery receiving the Aaronic and Melchizedek Priesthood.

RESTORATION OF
THE AARONIC PRIESTHOOD

During the early decades of the 19th century, the subject of Christian baptism was discussed and debated among the various religious denominations. Because the doctrine of baptism was misunderstood in the world, many people wondered who should receive it, if any Christian could perform the rite or only ordained ministers, and the manner of how it should be administered—either by pouring, sprinkling, or total immersion in water.

While translating the *Book of Mormon*, the Prophet and Oliver Cowdery discovered various passages in the ancient record which mentioned *baptism for the remission of sins*. Due to divergent teachings in various congregations regarding this rite, Joseph and Oliver decided to inquire of the Lord for knowledge on this important subject.

On May 15, 1829, the Prophet and Oliver Cowdery mutually agreed—and we may safely believe were prompted by the Spirit of the Lord—to go to a wooded area along the bank of the Susquehanna River, near Harmony, Pennsylvania, and pray to receive an answer concerning baptism.

While they were praying, an angelic messenger

silently descended in "a cloud of light," and said that his name was John, the same that is called John the Baptist in the New Testament. He said that he acted under the direction of Peter, James and John, who held the keys of the Melchizedek Priesthood, which Priesthood he said would in due time be conferred upon them. This same messenger told that he had been sent to confer on Joseph and Oliver the Aaronic Priesthood, which holds the keys of the temporal Gospel. John the Baptist then laid his hands upon their heads and ordained them by saying: "Upon you my fellow servants, in the name of Messiah I confer the Priesthood of Aaron, which holds the keys of the ministering of angels, and of the gospel of repentance, and of baptism by immersion for the remission of sins; and this shall never be taken again from the earth, until the sons of Levi do offer again an offering unto the Lord in righteousness"[135] (D&C 13).

This same John baptized our Lord in mortality by immersion in water (Matt. 3:13-17; Mark 1:9-11; Luke 2:21-22). "Baptism," says Elder McConkie, "means immersion. There was no thought of any other mode or form of baptism in the Church our Lord set up until after that holy organization had fallen prey to the doctrine of men and of devils."[136] This same angelic messenger was the last legal administrator, holding keys and authority under the Mosaic dispensation (D& C 84:26-28). "There is perfect order in the kingdom of God," says Elder Joseph Fielding Smith, "and he recognizes the authority of his servants. It was for this reason John, who acted under the direction of Peter, James, and John came to Joseph Smith and Oliver Cowdery and restored the Aaronic Priesthood, which John held in the dispensation of the meridian of time, and which became lost in the great apostasy because of . . . [the] corrupting of the Church of Jesus Christ."[137]

After these two men received the Aaronic Priesthood, this messenger instructed Joseph and Oliver to go down into the water of the Susquehanna River and baptize each other. After which they were to lay hands upon each other's head and re-confer the Priesthood which he had conferred upon them. From this we observe that the Aaronic Priesthood was conferred upon the Prophet and Oliver prior to them being baptized. Yet, the proper order in the Church is for an individual to be baptized, then for him to receive the Priesthood. To explain why this order was reversed, we rely upon the knowledge of Elder Joseph Fielding Smith. "There was no one living in mortality who held the keys of this Priesthood, therefore it was necessary that this messenger [John], who held the keys of the Aaronic Priesthood in the Dispensation of the Meridian of Time, should be sent to confer this power. It is contrary to the order of heaven for those who have passed beyond the veil to officiate and labor for the living on the earth, *only wherein mortal man cannot act, and thereby it becomes necessary for those who have passed through the resurrection to act for them.* Otherwise, John would have followed the regular order, which is practiced in the Church, and would have first baptized Joseph Smith and Oliver Cowdery and then conferred upon them the Aaronic Priesthood"[138] (Italics added).

As the angel had instructed these men, they entered the water and Joseph first baptized Oliver and then Oliver baptized Joseph. The Prophet says that immediately after coming out of the water, they each experienced great and glorious blessings from our

Heavenly Father. Being filled with the Holy Ghost, each of them began to give prophecy of the coming forth of the Church and the great work of the Lord in the latter days.

Following their baptism in the river, as instructed by John the Baptist, the Prophet laid his hands upon Oliver and ordained him to the Aaronic Priesthood, and afterwards Oliver laid his hands on Joseph and ordained him to this same Priesthood. Accordingly, they then followed the proper order of conferring priesthood. "For the first time in centuries," says Elder Joseph Fielding Smith, "there now stood on the earth *men with proper authority to officiate in baptism for the remission of sins*"[139] (Italics added).

With further explanation concerning the restoration of the Aaronic Priesthood, Elder Bruce R. McConkie has written: "Thus mortal men received both the lesser Priesthood and the keys to go with it. [Joseph and Oliver] received an endowment of heavenly power, together with the right to use it for the benefit and blessing of their fellowmen. They could now begin to preach the gospel; they could baptize for the remission of sins; but they could not confer the gift of the Holy Ghost. In due course, by the authority they then received, the sons of Levi will offer again their sacrificial performances before the Lord, as Malachi promised."[140]

Because of increased opposition, Joseph and Oliver were compelled to keep secret their ordination to the Aaronic Priesthood and baptism, excepting close family and friends whom they trusted. Soon, the promised Melchizedek Priesthood would be conferred upon the Prophet and Oliver Cowdery.

RESTORATION OF
THE MELCHIZEDEK PRIESTHOOD

As has been written in Chapter Four of this work, Elder Orson F. Whitney asked President Lorenzo Snow how Joseph Smith was able to see the Father and the Son and live, when he did not hold the Melchizedek Priesthood. President Snow replied: "Joseph did hold the priesthood; he came with it into the world."[141]

Likewise, President Joseph F. Smith of the First Presidency said: "Joseph Smith held the Melchizedek Priesthood before he came to the earth . . . *but it had to be reconfirmed upon him in the flesh by Peter, James, and John . . . .*"[142]

With this knowledge that the Prophet brought the Melchizedek Priesthood with him into mortality, but it had to be reconfirmed upon him, we learn that a short time after John the Baptist appeared to Joseph and Oliver, these same men received the Melchizedek Priesthood. Unfortunately, the actual date when this higher Priesthood was conferred is not recorded by the Prophet. Without going into a lengthy discussion on the subject, it has been determined that this great event transpired between May 15, 1829 and April, 1830.[143] In a published book by Hyrum L. Andrus, he says that "it probably came before July, 1829, for a revelation in June referred to Oliver Cowdery and David Whitmer as being called with the same calling as the Apostle Paul"[144] (D&C 18:9). According to Elder Joseph Fielding Smith, "it was only a few days after the first ordination."[145]

Concerning this glorious event, the Prophet testifies: "Peter, James, and John [came] in the wilderness between Harmony [Pennsylvania], Susquehanna river [and Colesville], declaring themselves as possessing the keys of the kingdom, and the dispensation of the fulness of times" (D&C 128:20). In another revelation given in August, 1830, we learn that the restoration of the Melchizedek Priesthood was under the hands of Peter, James, and John, "whom I have sent unto you, by whom I have ordained you and confirmed you to be apostles, and especial witnesses of my name" (D&C 27:12).

"Oliver Cowdery gave several testimonies of the above visitations," says Hyrum Andrus, "by John the Baptist and by Peter, James, and John. In an address at Council Bluffs, Iowa, October 29, 1848, he testified that he 'was present with Joseph Smith when a holy angel from God came down from heaven and conferred on us, or restored, the lesser or Aaronic Priesthood.' He also declared that he was 'present with Joseph Smith when the higher or Melchizedek Priesthood was conferred.'"[146]

On the appointed day, Peter, James, and John visited Joseph and Oliver and conferred the higher Priesthood and the keys upon them. Concerning this, Elder Bruce R.McConkie has written: " . . . by latter-day revelation we know that they held and restored 'the keys of the kingdom, which belong always unto the Presidency of the High Priesthood' (D&C 81:2), or in other words, they were the First Presidency in their day."[147] In another work, he wrote that these "heavenly ministrants conferred upon their mortal fellows the Melchizedek Priesthood, the keys of the kingdom of God, and the keys of the dispensation of the fulness of time (D& C 27:12-13)."[148]

Now that Joseph and Oliver received the Melchizedek Priesthood, they had keys and authority to organize the Church and administer the affairs of it.

"This higher Priesthood embraces within it the holy apostleship," says Elder McConkie, "and is the power by which the gospel and the Church are administered, and by which the gift of the Holy Ghost and salvation in its eternal fulness are made available to men, the recipients [who were the Prophet Joseph Smith and Oliver Cowdery] of so great a boon were able to organize the Church and kingdom of God on earth, which they did on the 6th of April in 1830."[149] Thus, the Prophet, who was told by John the Baptist that he would be called the "first Elder of the Church," and Oliver Cowdery, as "the second" were given important Priesthood keys to administer the affairs of the Lord's Church on earth.[150]

ELIJAH, MOSES, AND ELIAS RESTORE KEYS

Besides Peter, James, and John bestowing upon the Joseph and Oliver the keys of the kingdom, other heavenly messengers also appeared to them and bestowed important keys. Why? For as Elder Joseph Fielding Smith has explained: "All the keys of all dispensations had to be brought in order to fulfill the words of the prophets and the purposes of the Lord in bringing to pass a complete restoration of all things."[151] Because this is the great and final gospel dispensation, all of the prophets who have headed gospel dispensations from the days of Adam to the days of Peter, James, and John had to come and restore their keys upon the Prophet Joseph Smith. These prophets did come and each bestowed the authority and keys each held.

While in the Kirtland Temple on April 3, 1836 the Prophet Joseph Smith and Oliver Cowdery were visited by some of the dispensation heads. In turn, *Moses* first appeared and committed the keys of the gathering of Israel and the restoration of the ten tribes. Next, *Elias*, who lived in the days of Abraham, committed the dispensation of the gospel of Abraham, that is—the great commission given to Abraham that he and his seed had a right to the priesthood, the gospel, and eternal life. Then, *Elijah* appeared, who was spoken of by Malachi as having the authority to restore the keys of turning the hearts of the fathers to the children, and the hearts of the children to their fathers (D&C 110:11-16).

The Prophet Joseph Smith never revealed all of the places or dates when angelic ministrants appeared and restored their respective keys and authority. However, in an epistle to the Saints, Joseph says that Michael (who is Adam)[152], Gabriel (who is Noah)[153], Raphael (who is speculated to being Enoch—to restore the power for men to be translated)[154], and "divers [various] angels, from Michael or Adam down to the present time, all declaring their dispensation, their rights, their keys, their honors, their majesty and glory, and the power of their priesthood . . ." (D&C 128:21).

While speaking on the subject of the restoration of the gospel in this dispensation, President John Taylor said: "I know of what I speak for I was very well acquainted with him [the Prophet] and was with him a great deal during his life, *and was with him when he died.* The principles which he had, placed him in communications with the Lord, and not only with the Lord, *but with the ancient apostles and prophets*; such men, for instance as Abraham, Isaac, Jacob, Noah, Adam, Seth, Enoch [who perhaps is Raphael?] and Jesus and the Father, and the apostles that lived on this continent as well as those who lived on the Asiatic continent." President Taylor than gives this insightful comment: "*He seemed to be as familiar with these people as we are with one another.* Why? Because he had to introduce a dispensation which was called the dispensation of the fulness of times, and it was known as such by the ancient servants of God"¹⁵⁵ (Italics added).

Five years before he became the President of the Church, then Elder John Taylor said this in a General Conference: "And when Joseph Smith was raised up as a Prophet of God, Mormon, Moroni, Nephi and others of the ancient Prophets who formerly lived on this Continent . . . came to him and communicated to him certain principles pertaining to the Gospel."¹⁵⁶

Thus, Elder Taylor's statement supports, in part, what the Prophet has written in his epistle to the Saints that "divers [various] angels had come declaring their dispensation . . ." (D&C 128:21). From these various comments, we readily determine that Joseph Smith, Jr. ranks as one of the greatest prophets who has ever lived. He truly was blessed to see, talk with, and receive important instructions and keys from every angelic ministrant from Adam down to Peter, James, and John.

THE QUORUM OF THE TWELVE APOSTLES GIVEN THE KEYS

Word was sent to members of Zion's Camp [who consisted of several hundred men who journeyed a great distance to redeem Zion by collecting money and purchasing land] that a meeting was being held on February 14, 1835. On that day, the Prophet explained to those individuals who were present that the object of the meeting was to choose men for important positions in the ministry, to go forth and prune the vineyard for the last time. Then, he said that he had been commanded by the Lord to prepare for the calling of the Twelve Apostles, in fulfillment of a revelation given before the Church was organized (D&C 18). These twelve men were to be chosen from among those who journeyed in Zion's Camp, and the three witnesses to the Book of Mormon were to select and ordain them. Following the usual opening exercises and instruction, a recess was called for one hour. When the meeting commenced, the three witnesses selected the Twelve.[157]

When the original Twelve Apostles were ordained by the laying on of hands, they did not receive the keys of the kingdom that the Prophet held. It is important to point out that the doctrines of the kingdom were unfolded a little at a time, line upon line. However, on that day, the Lord declared that the Twelve were equal with the Presidency as a quorum. This is to say that if the First Presidency were taken away, the Twelve Apostles would direct the affairs of the Church until such time as the First Presidency should again be organized (D&C 107:21-24).

The following is written by Elder Joseph Fielding Smith, who received his information from *Times and Seasons*, Volume 5, p. 651: "The Lord . . . commanded the Prophet to confer upon the heads of the Twelve Apostles, *every key*, power, and principle, *that the Lord had sealed upon his head*. The Prophet declared that he knew not why, but the Lord commanded him to endow the Twelve with these keys and priesthood, and after it was done, he rejoiced very much, saying in substance, 'Now, if they kill me, you have all the keys and all the ordinances and you can confer them upon others, and the powers of Satan will not be able to tear down the kingdom as fast as you will be able to build it up, and upon your shoulders will the responsibility of leading this people rest."[158]

Substantiating what has been written by Elder Smith, we turn to the discourses of Wilford Woodruff, who became the fourth President of the Church, and read his words: "The Prophet Joseph, I am now satisfied, had a thorough [understanding] that [this] was the last meeting we [The First Presidency and Quorum of the Twelve Apostles] would hold together here in the flesh. We had had our endowments; we had had all the blessings sealed upon our heads that were ever given to the apostles or prophets on the face of the earth. On that occasion, the Prophet rose up and said to us: 'Brethren, I have desired to live to see this [Nauvoo] temple built. I shall never live to see it, but you will. I have sealed upon your heads all the keys of the kingdom of God. *I have sealed upon you every key, power, principle that the God of heaven has revealed to me.* Now, no matter where I may go or what I may do, the kingdom rests upon you' (Italics added).

". . . I am the last man living who heard that declaration . . .

"I say to the Latter-day Saints, the keys of the kingdom of God are here, and they are going to stay here, too, until the coming of the Son of Man . . . They may not rest upon my head but a short time, but they will then rest on the head of another apostle, and another after him, and so continue until the coming of the Lord Jesus Christ . . . ."[159]

From what has been presented, we know that

Priesthood and keys were bestowed upon the Prophet Joseph Smith by angelic ministrants. Prior to his death, he bestowed those same keys upon the Quorum of the Twelve Apostles. Concerning the restoration of these keys, powers, and authority, we declare that they are now held by the First Presidency and the Quorum of the Twelve Apostles who preside over The Church of Jesus Christ of Latter-day Saints. They will continue to be held by these chosen servants, until the coming of our Lord Jesus Christ, who will personally reign for a thousand years upon this earth.

CHAPTER TWELVE
MARVELOUS EXPERIENCES
NEAR CUMORAH

JOSEPH AND OLIVER ENTERED
THE HILL CUMORAH

For reasons of his own, the Prophet Joseph Smith never recorded every sacred or marvelous event that transpired in his life. Fortunately for us, some of these experiences have been related by family members or early Church leaders.

Following his unsuccessful attempt to translate a portion of the *Book of Mormon*, Oliver Cowdery was told by the Lord that "*other records* have I, that I will give unto you power that you may assist to translate" (D&C 9: 2) (Italics added). Concerning these *other records*, we turn our attention to a special conference held at Farmington, Utah, on June 17, 1877, where President Brigham Young told the Saints of a fascinating experience that Joseph and Oliver had at the Hill Cumorah.

"I lived right in the country where the plates were found from which the *Book of Mormon* was translated, and I know a great many things pertaining to that country. I believe I will take the liberty to tell you of another circumstance that will be *marvelous as anything can be*. This is an incident in the life of Oliver Cowdery, but he did not take the liberty of telling such things in meeting as I take."

President Young then gave his reason for relating this story:

"I tell these things to you, and *I have a motive for doing so*. I want to carry them to the ears of my brethren and sisters and to the children also, that they may grow to an understanding of some things that *seem to be entirely hidden from the human family*. Oliver Cowdery went with the Prophet Joseph when he deposited these plates [of the *Book of Mormon*]. Joseph did not translate all of the plates; there was a portion of them sealed, which you can learn from the Book of *Doctrine and Covenants*. When Joseph got the plates, the angel [Moroni] instructed him to carry them back to the *hill Cumorah*, which he did."

President Young tells what happened when Oliver Cowdery and the Prophet went to this place:

"Oliver says that when Joseph and Oliver went there, *the hill opened*, and they walked into a cave, *in which there was a large and spacious room*. He says he did not think, at the time, whether they had the light of the sun or artificial light; but that it was just as light as day. They laid the plates on the table; it was a large table that stood in the room. Under this table there was a pile of plates as much as two feet high, and there were altogether in this room more plates than probably many wagon loads; they were piled up in the corners and along the walls."

Then, President Young speaks of another ancient item that these two men saw:

"The first time they went there the *sword of Laban* hung upon the wall; but when they went again it had been taken down and laid upon the table across the gold plates [of the *Book of Mormon*]; it was unsheathed, and on it was written these words: 'This sword will never be sheathed again until the kingdoms of this world become the kingdom of our God and his Christ.'

"I tell you this as coming not only from Oliver Cowdery, but others who were familiar with it, and who understand it just as well as we understand coming to this meeting . . . *I take this liberty of referring to those things so that they will not be forgotten and lost . . .*

"Now you may think I am unwise in publicly telling these things, thinking perhaps I should preserve them in my own breast; but such is not my mind. I would like the people called Latter-day Saints to understand some little things with regard to the workings and dealings of the Lord with his people here upon the earth"[160] (Italics added).

COMMENTS BY
PRESIDENT HEBER C. KIMBALL

In support of President Young's statement that others were familiar with this story, President Heber C. Kimball, First Counselor to President Young, briefly spoke of this incident 21 years previously. At a gathering of the Saints at the Salt Lake City Bowery on September 28, 1856, he says:

"Brother Mills mentioned in his song, that crossing the Plains with handcarts was one of the greatest events that ever transpired in this Church. I will admit that it is an important event, successfully testing another method for gathering Israel, but its importance is small in comparison with the visitation of the angel of God to the Prophet Joseph, and with the reception of the sacred records from the hand of Moroni at the hill Cumorah.

"How does it compare with the vision that Joseph

and others had, *when they went into a cave in the hill Cumorah, and saw more records than ten men could carry?* There were books piled up on tables, book upon book. Those records this people will yet have, if they accept of the *Book of Mormon* and observe its precepts, and keep the commandments."[161]

A LETTER OF
PRESIDENT JOSEPH F. SMITH

Not only did Heber C. Kimball have knowledge of this cave in the hill, but President Joseph F. Smith, Second Counselor to President Wilford Woodruff, also had been informed of it. In a letter to Elder Edward Stevenson, dated December 5, 1889, President Smith asked him if he had any knowledge of the room in the Hill Cumorah. Then, President Smith says: "All I know about the matter is what Pres. B. Young related to me, many years ago when I commenced speaking to the Y.M.M.I. Associations on the early history of the Church.

"He told me that the Hill opened, as it were, to Joseph, and Oliver . . . and they saw—as it appeared to them—a chamber containing all the Plates and Records of the Nephites, with the *Sword of Laban*, the *Breast Plate*, the *Director*, the *Interpreters* . . . "[162] (Italics added).

Though Presidents Young and Kimball did not mention these other items, we learn from this letter of President Smith's that besides seeing the plates and the Sword of Laban, that Oliver Cowdery and the Prophet Joseph Smith also saw in this cave the Breast Plate, the Liahona, and the Urim and Thummim.

Whether or not that cave or chamber is still within

the Hill Cumorah, we are not informed. Because it was there when the Prophet and Oliver Cowdery went there twice, we may properly believe that it is still there.

AN EXPERIENCE OF
ORRIN PORTER ROCKWELL

In the same sermon that President Brigham Young related the account of the Hill Cumorah opening and Joseph and Oliver entering the cave, President Young tells of another marvelous experience, one that Orrin Porter Rockwell had near that same hill. "He was with certain parties that lived *nearby where the plates were found* that contain the records of the *Book of Mormon.* There were a great many treasures hid up by the Nephites. Porter was with them one night where there were treasures, and they could find them easy enough, but they could not obtain them.

"I will tell you a story which will be marvelous to most of you. It was told me by Porter, *whom I would believe just as quickly as any man that lives.* When he tells a thing he understands, he will tell it just as he knows it; *he is a man that does not lie.* He said on this night, when they were engaged hunting for this old treasure, they dug around the end of a chest for some twenty inches. The chest was about three feet square. One man, who was determined to have the contents of the chest, took his pick and struck into the lid of it, and split through into the chest. The blow took off a piece of the lid, which a certain lady kept in her possession until she died. That chest of money went into the bank [embankment]. Porter describes it so (making a rumbling sound); he says this is just as true as the heavens are. I have heard others tell the same story. *I relate this because it is marvelous to you. But to those who understand these things, it is not marvelous*"[163] (Italics added).

EXPERIENCES OF DAVID WHITMER

As has been previously written in this work, David Whitmer became one of the Three Witnesses to the *Book of Mormon*. The following events transpired before he became one of those witnesses.

Due to increased opposition in Harmony, Pennsylvania, it was determined by the Prophet that the work of translating the *Book of Mormon* could no longer continue there at his in-laws' home. Oliver Cowdery wrote to a young friend, David Whitmer, who lived at Fayette, New York, and to whom he had previously written concerning the coming forth of the *Book of Mormon*. In this letter Oliver asked David to come to Harmony and take the Prophet and his wife, and himself to the Whitmer home, where David's parents lived with several children. This request found David Whitmer in the middle of spring farming. He had twenty acres of land to plow and concluded to do that before journeying to Harmony. Several years later, he related the following experience to Elders Orson Pratt and Joseph F. Smith:

"I got up one morning to go to work as usual and on going to the field, found that between five and seven acres of my land had been plowed under during the night. I don't know who did it, but it was done just as I would have done it myself, and the plow was left standing in the furrow. This enabled me to start sooner."[164]

Besides this miraculous assistance, he tells of

harrowing in a field of wheat before going to Harmony and being surprised that he had accomplished more work in a few hours than was usual to do in two or three days.

A day later, he went to spread plaster over a field—though we are not informed of what plaster is, it was according to the custom of the farmers in that area—and was again surprised to find it well done. David's sister, who lived near the field, told him that three unknown men had appeared in the field the day before and spread the plaster with great skill. She thought that David had hired these men to do this work.[165]

When David traveled to Harmony, he was met some distance from the town by the Prophet and Oliver. "Oliver told me that Joseph had informed him when I started from home, where I stopped the first night, how I read the sign at the tavern, where I stopped the next night . . . and that I would be there that day before dinner, and this is why they had come out to meet me. All of which was exactly as Joseph had told Oliver, at which I was greatly astonished."[166]

The following was related by David Whitmer to Elders Pratt and Smith: "When I was returning to Fayette, with Joseph and Oliver, all of us riding in the wagon, Oliver and I on an old fashioned wooden spring-seat, and Joseph behind us—when traveling along in a clear, open space, a very pleasant, nice-looking old man suddenly appeared by the side of our wagon and saluted us with, 'Good morning; it is very warm,' at the same time wiping his face or forehead with his hand. We returned the salutation, and by a sign from Joseph, I invited him to ride, if he was going our way. But he said very pleasantly, '*No, I am going to Cumorah.*' This name was somewhat new to me, and I did not know what Cumorah meant. We all gazed at him and at each other, and as I looked round inquiringly at Joseph, the old man instantly disappeared, so that I did not see him again."

Elder Joseph F. Smith asked: "Did you notice his appearance?"

David replied: "I should think I did. He was, I should think, about five feet eight or nine inches tall and heavyset . . . His hair and beard were white, like Brother Pratt's, but his beard was not so heavy. I also remember that he had on his back a sort of knapsack with something in it, shaped like a book."[167]

When David, Joseph, Emma, and Oliver arrived at the Whitmer home, Mr. Peter Whitmer, who was the father of David, kindly received them and was anxious and willing to know more concerning the work of translating the *Book of Mormon*. Joseph, Emma, and Oliver received their boarding free at the Whitmer home and every courtesy was extended to them by members of the Whitmer family.

MRS. WHITMER SEES THE PLATES

David Whitmer relates another experience that happened shortly after the Prophet, Emma, and Oliver arrived. He says he saw something in his father's barn which led him to believe that it was the plates. He frankly asked the Prophet if it was so; Joseph replied that it was.

In addition, he says that one day as his mother went to milk cows, she was met by this same old man who had said he was going to Cumorah and he said to her: "You have been very faithful and diligent in your labors, but you are tired because of the increase of your toil; it is proper, therefore, that you should receive a witness, that your faith may be strengthened." He then showed Mrs. Whitmer the plates.[168]

In another account of Mrs. Whitmer seeing the plates, published in the *Millennial Star* by a person who only put their initials of E. S., it is implied that this old man was one of the Three Nephites.[169] However, it appears from David's version, that this old man was the Angel Moroni, who was going to the Hill Cumorah with the plates in his knapsack.

ZELPH

According to instruction, a call went forth asking for volunteers to go to Zion to redeem it. The Prophet led this group of people, called Zion's Camp. Their journey took them through Dayton, Indianapolis, Springfield and Jacksonville, Illinois, and across the Mississippi River into Missouri. Near the banks of the Illinois River, west of Jacksonville, the Prophet says that they "visited several of the mounds which had been thrown up by the ancient inhabitants of this country—Nephites, Lamanites, etc. . . ."

On one of those mounds some men took a shovel and hoe and removed the dirt down about a foot and discovered the skeleton of a man, almost in his entirety, and between his ribs was the stone point of a Lamanite arrow. It was revealed to the Prophet that "the person whose skeleton was before us was a white Lamanite, a large, thick-set man, and a man of God. His name was Zelph. He was a warrior and chieftain under the great prophet Onandagus, *who was known from the Hill Cumorah* . . . He was killed in battle by the arrow found among his ribs, during the last great struggle of the Lamanites and Nephites"[170] (Italics added).

From these various narratives we gain a great appreciation for marvelous experiences near Cumorah. This truly is a sacred place that was prepared by the Lord for bringing forth the Dispensation of the Fulness of Times.

TESTIMONIES OF SACRED EVENTS NEAR CUMORAH

In concluding our study of marvelous experiences near Cumorah, we again repeat what President Heber C. Kimball said: " . . . its importance [crossing the Plains] is small in comparison with the visitation of the angel of God to the Prophet Joseph Smith, and with the reception of the sacred records from the hand of Moroni at the hill Cumorah."[171] In this author's estimation, President Kimball should have also listed the appearance of the Father and Son to the boy-prophet in the Sacred Grove. This is the paramount visit. Concerning what happened in this grove of trees, located approximately three miles from the Hill Cumorah, the Prophet declares: "I had actually seen a light, and in the midst of that light, I saw two Personages, and they did in reality speak to me; and though I was hated and persecuted for saying that I had seen a vision, *yet it was true* . . . I knew it, and I knew that God knew it . . ." (Joseph Smith—History 1: 25) (Italics added).

From what has been written in this work, I, too, add my testimony that God lives, and Jesus is the Christ, and that the boy-prophet actually saw the Father and the Son in the Sacred Grove. In addition, Joseph Smith, Jr. is a prophet of God who obtained the plates from Moroni on the Hill Cumorah, and through instruments of revelation, he translated the Book of Mormon. This knowledge truly is *Glad Tidings Near Cumorah*!

ENDNOTES

CHAPTER ONE

1 Bruce R. McConkie, *Mormon Doctrine*, 2nd ed., Bookcraft, 1966, p. 742; See the author's book, *Mysteries of the Kingdom*, 2001, pp. 13-19.

2 Gen. 2, 3; Moses 3, 4.

3 *Doctrines of Salvation, Sermons and Writings of Joseph Fielding Smith*, Compiled by Bruce R. McConkie, Volume 3, p. 74. See also Gen. 1: 9-10.

4 *Historical Record*, Jenson, Vol. 7 and 8, p. 432; *Life of Heber C. Kimball*, Whitney, p. 219 (1888 ed.); Alvin R. Dyer, *The Refiners Fire*, Deseret Book, 1969, p. 111.

5 *Life of John D. Lee*, p. 91, as printed in *The Refiners Fire*, p. 110.

6 *Doctrines of Salvation*, Vol. 3, p. 77; D&C 57: 1-3.

7 *Deseret News*, 10-25, 1895 (Letter Benjamin F. Johnson); Alvin R. Dyer, *The Refiners Fire*, Deseret Book, 1969, pp. 111, 167.

8 Bruce R. McConkie, *Mormon Doctrine*, 2nd ed., Bookcraft, 1966, pp. 20-21.

9 James E. Talmage, *Jesus the Christ*, 1962 ed., pp. 610-611.

10 Ibid., p. 620.

11 Bruce R. McConkie, *The Mortal Messiah: From Bethlehem to Calvary*, Book 4, Deseret Book, p. 125. Used by permission.

12 Joseph Fielding Smith, *Essentials in Church History*, 1964 ed., pp. 38-40.

13 *Joseph Smith—History*, Extracts from the *History of Joseph Smith, the Prophet*, verses 5-14; *Documentary History of the Church*, Vol. 1, pp. 2-5.

14 B. H. Roberts, *A Comprehensive History of the Church*, Vol. 1, p. 53.

15 *Encyclopedia of Mormonism*, Vol. 3, *Sacred Grove*.

16 Ibid., *A Comprehensive History of The Church*, Vol. 1, p. 42.

17 George Albert Smith, *Conference Report*, April 1906, p. 52-56.

18 *Encyclopedia of Mormonism*, Vol. 3, *Sacred Grove*.

19 Elder Thomas E. McKay, *Conference Report*, April 1949, p. 35.

CHAPTER TWO

20 Elder Bruce R. McConkie, *A New Witness for the Articles of Faith*, Deseret Book, 1985, p. 3.

21 Ibid., p. 4.

22 Joseph Fielding Smith, comp., *Teachings of theProphet Joseph Smith*, 1968 ed., p. 365.

23 Elder Bruce R. McConkie, *A New Witness for the Articles of Faith*, Deseret Book, 1985, p. 5.

24 Elder Boyd K. Packer, *That All May Be Edified*, Bookcraft, 1982, p. 14.

25 Elder Bruce R. McConkie, *A New Witness for the Articles of Faith*, Deseret Book, 1985, p. 5.

26 Elder Boyd K. Packer, *That All May Be Edified*, Bookcraft, 1982, p. 13.

27 Charles W. Nibley, Second Counselor in the First Presidency, *Conference Report*, April 6, 1830, pp. 26-27.

28 Leon M. Strong, *Three Timely Treasures*, p. 15—Copyright 1949.

29 An address, February 3, 1980, *Joseph Smith Memorial Lecture*, p. 2; *Conference Report*, April 5, 1974, page 4; *Conference Report*, April 4, 1975, pp. 3-4; *Conference Report*, April 6, 1973, p. 4. A counselor in the First Presidency, Charles W. Nibley, also states that it was the sixth of April when Christ was born—See *Conference Report*, April 6, 1930, pp. 26-27. See also the author's book, *Mary, Mother of Jesus*, pp. 88-89.

30 See D&C 21, and Joseph Fielding Smith, *Essentials in Church History*, pp. 90-94.

31 Bruce R. McConkie, *Mormon Doctrine*, 2nd ed., p. 290.

CHAPTER THREE

32 George Q. Cannon, *Life of Joseph Smith*, first edition, 1888, pp. 36-37.

33 Elder Orson Pratt, *Journal of Discourses*, Volume 12, p. 354.

34 Elder Orson Pratt, *Journal of Discourses*, Volume 17, p. 279, delivered on September 20, 1874.

35 George Q. Cannon, *Life of Joseph Smith*, first edition, 1888, pp. 36-37.

36 B. H. Roberts, *Journal of Discourses*, Volume 25, p. 138.

CHAPTER FOUR

37 President Heber J. Grant, An Address to Seminary Teachers, given July 13, 1934, *Teach That Which Encourages Faith*, pp. 14-15 (From a 20 page pamplet).

38 President George Q. Cannon, *Journal of Discourses*, Volume 24, page 372.

39 President Brigham Young, *Journal of Discourses*, Volume 16, p. 31.

40 Elder Joseph Fielding Smith, *Conference Report*, October 3, 1936, pp. 60-61.

41 Elder Orson Pratt, *Millennial Star*, 11: 238, August 1, 1849.

42 Elder Spencer W. Kimball, *Faith Precedes the Miracle*, Deseret Book, 1972, pp. 86 and 88.

43 *Doctrines of Salvation, Sermons and Writings of Joseph Fielding Smith*, Compiled by Bruce R. McConkie, Volume 1, pp. 42-43.

44 Bruce R. McConkie, *Doctrinal New Testament Commentary*, Volume 3, p. 227.

45 Elder Orson F. Whitney, *Gospel Themes*, pp. 78-79, December, 1913.

46 Elder Orson F. Whitney, *Conference Report*, October 8, 1905, p. 93.

47 Elder Joseph Fielding Smith, a personal letter to Neil H. Purdie, dated January 3, 1947. Photocopy of the original letter in possession.

48 President Joseph F. Smith, Second Counselor to President John Taylor, *Personal Letterbooks*, p. 144, LDS Church Archives, MS f 271, Film Reel #3, Book #2.

49 Joseph Fielding Smith, *The Improvement Era*, 38: 208-209, April, 1935.

CHAPTER FIVE

50 Elder Joseph Fielding Smith, *Church News*, September 5, 1931, p. 2, also reprinted in *Doctrines of Salvation*, Volume 1, p. 199.

51 *The Discourses of Wilford Woodruff*, pp. 284-285.

52 *History of Joseph Smith, by His Mother, Lucy Mack Smith*, edited by Preston Nibley. There are various editions—1845, 1853, 1865, 1900, and 1901. Out of print for 44 years, it was reprinted by Bookcraft, 1958, pp. 79-80.

53 President J. Reuben Clark, *On the Way to Immortality and Eternal Life*, Deseret Book, 1949, p. 122.

CHAPTER SIX

54 Boyd K. Packer, *A Watchman on the Tower*, by Lucille C. Tate, Deseret Book, 1995, p. 181.

55 Oliver Cowdery, *Messenger and Advocate*, in 1834, and recorded in *Documentary History of the Church*, Volume 1, page 15.

56 *Doctrines of Salvation, Sermons and Writings of Joseph Fielding Smith*, Compiled by Bruce R. McConkie, Volume 3, p. 232.

57 Ibid., p. 233.

58 Ibid., pp. 233-234.

59 Ibid., pp. 234-243.

60 A. P. Kesler, *Young Woman's Journal*, 9: 73, February 1898.

61 Elder George Q. Cannon, Editor, *The Juvenile Instructor*, 8: 108, July 5, 1873.

62 Brother Andrew Jenson, *Conference Report*, April 8, 1917, p. 99.

63 Oliver Cowdery, *Messenger and Advocate*, October 1835, p. 198.

CHAPTER SEVEN

64 *Documentary History of the Church*, Volume 4, p. 537.

65 *History of Joseph Smith, by His Mother, Lucy Mack Smith*, pp. 81-83.

66 John Taylor, *Messenger and Advocate*, June 1837, pp. 513-514.

67 *History of Joseph Smith, by His Mother, Lucy Mack Smith*, pp. 83-84.

68 Ibid., p. 85.

69 Ibid., pp. 99-101.

70 Paul E. Gilbert & Douglas L. Powell, *Near Cumorah's Hill, Images of the Restoration*, Covenant Communications, 2000, p. 47. Information taken from H. Donl Peterson, *Moroni: Joseph Smith's Teacher*, in *Regional Studies*, p. 63.

71 Elam Cheney, Sr., *Young Woman's Journal*, 17: 539-540. Dec. 1906.

72 *Stories About Joseph Smith*, by Edwin F. Parry, pp. 14-15.

73 President Joseph F. Smith, President of the Church, Personal Letterbooks, p. 247, LDS Church Archives—Ms f 271, Film Reel #13, Book #1.

74 *History of Joseph Smith, by His Mother, Lucy Mack Smith*, p. 102.

75 Ibid., pp. 102-104.

76 Ibid., p. 110.

77 Ibid., pp. 107-108.

78 Ibid., p. 109.

79 Ibid., p. 111.

CHAPTER EIGHT

80 *History of Joseph Smith, by His Mother, Lucy Mack Smith*, p. 111

81 Ibid., p. 112.

82 Pearson H. Corbett, *Hyrum Smith—Patriarch*, Deseret Book, 1963, pp. 39 and 452.

83 Scott and Maurine Proctor, eds., *The Revised and Enhanced History of Joseph Smith by His Mother* (Salt Lake City: Bookcraft, 1966, 81. As quoted in *Near Cumorah's Hill*, p. 47. Also written by President Joseph F. Smith, Sixth President of the Church, from *Personal Letterbooks*, pp. 395-396, LDS Church Archives—Ms f 271, Film Reel #4, Book #2.

84 Parley P. Pratt, *Voice of Warning*, 1837, p. 92.

85 Elder Orson Pratt, *Journal of Discourses*, Volume 19, p. 214.

86 Bruce R. McConkie, *Mormon Doctrine*, 2nd. ed., Bookcraft, 1966, p. 818.

87 Elder John Taylor, *Journal of Discourses*, Volume 24, pp. 262-263, June 24, 1883.

88 *History of Joseph Smith, by His Mother, Lucy Mack Smith*, pp. 104, 107, and 110.

89 President Joseph F. Smith, *Personal Letterbooks*, pp. 395-396, LDS Church Archives—Ms f 271, Film Reel #4, Book #2.

90 *Documentary History of the Church*, Volume 1, p. 19, Volume 3, p. 28, and Volume 4, p. 537.

91 David Whitmer, *Address to All Believers in Christ*, a pamphlet published by David Whitmer, 1887, p. 12. As printed in *A Comprehensive History of the Church*, Volume 1, p. 128.

92 See Tucker's *Origin, Rise and Progress of Mormonism*, chapter 2. As printed in *A Comprehensive History of the Church*, Vol. 1, p. 129.

93 *Messenger and Advocate*, Volume 1, p. 14; October 1834. As printed as a footnote in Joseph Smith—History 1, p. 58.

94 *A Comprehensive History of the Church*, Volume 1, p. 130.

CHAPTER NINE

95 *A Comprehensive History of the Church*, Volume 1, pp. 88-90.

96 *History of Joseph Smith, by His Mother, Lucy Mack Smith*, pp. 112-113.

97 Elder B. H. Roberts, *Defense of the Faith and the Saints*, 1907, Volume 1, p. 257.

98 *Priddy Meeks, His Journal*, p. 32. He was born in 1795. He was a physician and surgeon; he says that he was writing Journal by memory in 1879.

99 Brigham Young, Council of the Twelve, *Manuscript History of Brigham Young*, December 27, 1841.

100 Matthias Cowley, *Wilford Woodruff, History of his Life and Labors*, p. 157, September 1909.

101 *Documentary History of the Church*, Volume 1, pp. 18-19.

102 Elder B. H. Roberts, *Defense of the Faith and the Saints*, 1: 257-259, 1907.

103 Joseph Fielding Smith, *Essentials in Church History*, p. 554.

104 Andrew Jenson, *Historical Record*, p. 216; *Seer Stones*, p. 15 by Ogden Kraut.

105 *A Comprehensive History of the Church*, Volume 1, p.128.

106 B. H. Roberts, *Defense of the Faith and the Saints*, Volume 1, pp. 283-285, 1907.

107 Ibid., pp. 259-260.

108 Elder Orson F. Whitney, *Saturday Night Thoughts*, p. 224, Revised Edition, 1927.

109 *Comprehensive History of the Church*, Volume 2, p. 100, (1930); originally published in the *Millennial Star*, Volume 40, p. 787, December 16, 1878.

110 David Whitmer, *An Address to All Believers*, a pamphlet, originally published in 1887.

111 *Wilford Woodruff's Journal*, Volume 8, p. 500; May 18, 1888. See also *A Comprehensive History of the Church*, Volume 6, p. 230. See also, Joseph Fielding Smith, *Doctrines of Salvation*, Volume 3, p. 225.

112 Joseph F. Smith, of the First Presidency, *Personal Letterbooks*, p. 438, LDS Church Archives—Ms f 271. Film Reed #3, Book #2.

113 *A Comprehensive History of the Church*, Volume 6, p. 231; See also Joseph Fielding Smith, *Doctrines of Salvation*, Volume 3, p. 225.

114 Elder Joseph Fielding Smith, *Doctrines of Salvation*, Volume 3, pp. 225-226.

CHAPTER TEN

115 Elder Joseph Fielding Smith, *Doctrines of Salvation*, Volume 1, pp. 205 and 210.

116 Elder Bruce R. McConkie, *Mormon Doctrine*, 2nd ed., p. 436.

117 *Documentary History of the Church*, Volume 1, pp. 52-53.

118 Elder Joseph Fielding Smith, *Doctrines of Salvation*, Volume 3, p. 218.

119 *A Comprehensive History of the Church*, Volume 1, p. 120 and 134.

120 *History of Joseph Smith, by His Mother, Lucy Mack Smith*, pp. 151-152.

121 *Documentary History of the Church*, Volume 1, pp. 53-54.

122 Ibid., p. 54.

123 Ibid., pp. 54-55.

124 Ibid., p. 55.

125 Andrew Jensen, *Historical Record*, p. 208, as written in the *Doctrine and Covenants Commentary*, Revised Edition, 1951, pp. 80-81. See also George Q. Cannon, *Juvenile Instructor*, 19 (1184): 107. See also *Encyclopedia of Mormonism*, Volume 4, *Visions of Joseph Smith*.

126 *Documentary History of the Church*, Volume 4, p. 537. This description was also published in *Times and Seasons* 3: 307, March 1, 1842.

127 Elder Orson Pratt, *Journal of Discourses*, Volume 7, p. 31.

128 Testimony of William Smith, as printed in *Millennial Star,* 56: 132, February 26, 1894.

129 B. F. Cummings, Editor, *Liahona, The Elders' Journal*, Volume 6, pp. 108-109, No. 5, July 18, 1908.

130 *History of Joseph Smith, by His Mother, Lucy Mack Smith*, pp. 152-153.

131 Joseph Fielding Smith, *Essentials in Church History*, Nineteenth Edition, 1964, pp. 80-81.

CHAPTER ELEVEN

132 *Teachings of the Prophet Joseph Smith*, p. 180.

133 President Joseph F. Smith, *Conference Report*, October 6, 1903, p. 87.

134 *Documentary History of the Church*, Volume 4, p. 207.

135 Ibid., Volume 1, pp. 39-40. See Joseph Fielding Smith, *Essentials*

in Church History, pp. 67-68.

136 Bruce R. McConkie, *Doctrinal New Testament Commentary*, Bookcraft, 1972, p. 124.

137 Joseph Fielding Smith, *Doctrines of Salvation*, Volume 3, pp. 89-90.

138 Joseph Fielding Smith, *Essentials in Church History*, p. 68.

139 Ibid., p. 69.

140 Bruce R. McConkie, *The Millennial Messiah*, Deseret Book, 1982, p. 118.

141 Elder Orson F. Whitney, *Conference Report*, October 8, 1905, p. 93.

142 President Joseph F. Smith, Of the First Presidency, *Personal Letterbooks*, LDS Church Archives—MS f 271, Film Reel #3, Book #2.

143 *A Comprehensive History of the Church*, Volume 1, pp. 183-184; *Documentary History of the Church*, Volume 1, Footnote, pp 40-43.

144 Hyrum L. Andrus, *Joseph Smith, the Man and the Seer*, Deseret Book, 1960, p. 84.

145 Joseph Fielding Smith, *Essentials in Church History*, p. 69.

146 Hyrum L. Andrus, *Joseph Smith, the Man and the Seer*, Deseret Book, 1960, p. 84. It was originally published in the *Deseret News*, April 13, 1859.

147 Bruce R. McConkie, *Doctrinal New Testament Commentary: The Gospels*, Volume 1, Bookcraft, 1965, p. 402.

148 Bruce R. McConkie, *A New Witness for the Articles of Faith*, Deseret Book, 1985, p. 321.

149 Ibid., pp. 321-322.

150 *Documentary History of the Church*, Volume 1, pp. 40-41.

151 *Doctrines of Salvation*, Volume 3, p. 125.

152 *Teachings of the Prophet Joseph Smith*, p. 157.

153 Ibid., p. 157.

154 Bruce R. McConkie, *Mormon Doctrine*, 2nd ed., p. 618.

155 President John Taylor, President of the Church, *Journal of Discourses*, Volume 21, p. 94. See also Volume 21, p. 65.

156 Elder Wilford Woodruff, *Journal of Discourses*, Volume 17, p. 374.

157 *Documentary History of the Church*, Volume 2, pp. 180-187.

158 Joseph Fielding Smith, *Doctrines of Salvation*, Volume 1, p. 259.

159 *Discourses of Wilford Woodruff*, pp. 71-73. This was originally printed in *Millennial Star*, 52: 755-757, 1880.

CHAPTER TWELVE

160 President Brigham Young, *Journal of Discourses*, Volume 19, p. 38; June 17, 1877.

161 President Heber C. Kimball, *Journal of Discourses*, Volume 4, p. 105.

162 President Joseph F. Smith, *Personal Letterbooks*, pp. 396-3l97, LDS Church Archives-Ms f 271, Film Reel #4, Book #2.

163 President Brigham Young, *Journal of Discourses*, Volume 19, pp. 37-38; June 17, 1877.

164 Pratt and Smith report, *Millennial Star*, Volume 11, pp. 769-774. Also in *A Comprehensive History of the Church*, Volume 1, p. 126.

165 George Q. Cannon, *Life of Joseph Smith*, pp. 57-68. Also in *A Comprehensive History of the Church*, Volume 1, p. 126.

166 *Millennial Star*, Volume 40, pp. 769-774.

167 Ibid, p. 772. Also in Andrew Jenson, *Historical Record*, p. 209. Also in *Doctrines of Salvation*, Volume 3, pp. 236-237. Also in *A Comprehensive History of the Church*, Volume 1, pp. 126-127.

168 Ibid., p. 772. Also in *A Comprehensive History of the Church*, Volume 1, p. 127.

169 *Millennial Star*, 49: 254, April 18, 1887. See the author's book, *The Three Nephites and Other Translated Beings*, pp. 52-53.

170 *Documentary History of the Church*, Volume 2, p. 79. See also *Essentials in Church History*, pp. 170-172.

171 President Heber C. Kimball, *Journal of Discourses*, Vol. 4, p. 105.

Index

Aaronic Priesthood, explanation concerning, 109-111; restoration of the, by John the Baptist, 111-114

Abraham,foreordained before born on earth was, 11; grand vision of intelligences shown to, 11; a great gospel dispensation presided over by, 12

Accounts, The Prophet Joseph Smith related various, of the First Vision, 20-26

Adam, born on this earth was, 1; Garden of Eden was where, and Eve lived, 1; all the land was in one place when, and Eve lived on the earth, 1 the land of America is where, and Eve lived, 1; Eve and, traveled 85 miles to live in Adam-ondi-Ahman, 2; great council to be held by, at Adam-ondi-Ahman, 2-3; angel in Gethsemane probably was, 4; Michael is also, 118; Joseph Smith was visited by, 118

Adam-ondi-Ahman, Adam and Eve traveled 85 miles to live in, 2; large land area comprised, 2, Christ established the foundations of, 2; Spring Hill Missouri included in the land of, 2; Far West Missouri included in the land of, 2; Adam to hold a great council at, 2; all who held keys will give accounting to Adam at, 2; Christ will come to, and receive back the keys, 2-3

Agency, Joseph Smith was allowed his, 15; one of greatest gifts is, 15

Answers, directions and, will come by different means, 14; Elder Packer explains how, can come, 14

April 6, President Charles Nibley believed, is the beautiful spring day Joseph entered the woods to pray, 16; birth of our Lord was on, 17; death of our Lord was on, 17-18; April Conference of Church held on or near, 18

Baptism, different ways of performing, 111; remission of sins by, 111; Elder McConkie's meaning of, 112

Baptist, John the, Joseph Smith and Oliver Cowdery were visited by, 111-112; under the direction of Peter and James and John, restored the Aaronic Priesthood, 112

Book of Mormon, Joseph Smith told and shown in vision the plates that would be translated into the, 46; how Joseph Smith translated the, 81-84; dates to translate, 98

Box, at Hill Cumorah Joseph

physical attributes of the, 33-34; four ways how Joseph Smith saw the, 35-40

Father, Elder Packer tells of importance of role of earthly, 53; Nephi asks his, where to obtain food, 53-54; Joseph Smith commanded by Moroni to tell his, of Moroni's visits and instructions, 50; Joseph Smith tells his, of visits and instructions by Moroni, 51; Joseph Smith told to obey instructions of Moroni by his, 51

Fire, Father and Son appeared to Prophet Joseph Smith in a pillar of light and, 25-27

First Vision, events that led to the, 6-7; greatest vision ever given to mortal man is, 16; Joseph Smith related various accounts of, 20-26; great persecution came to Joseph Smith for relating, 21-22; Father and Son appeared in a pillar of light and fire to Joseph Smith in, 24-29; doctrines learned from, 40; to Methodist preacher Joseph Smith related, 32

Foreordained, Lord's chosen servants are, 11; Jeremiah was, 11, Abraham was, 11; Joseph Smith was, 12

Gabriel, another name for Noah is, 118; Joseph Smith was visited by, 118

Garden of Eden, paradisiacal in nature was, 1; several acres comprised, 1; Jackson County, Missouri is location of, 1; Temple Block in Jackson County identical spot where, was 2; City Zion or New Jerusalem to be built where, was located 2; Joseph Smith dedicated site for the temple in Independence Missouri where, was located, 2; Adam and Eve were expelled from, 2; at Second Coming earth will be similar as it was in the, 3

Garden of Gethsemane, Jesus and his disciples entered the, 3; olive orchard known as, 3; Jesus in company with Peter and James and John spent several agonizing hours in, 3-4; an angel appeared to our Lord in the, 4; second Eden is referred as, 4; our Lord's redemptive sacrifice occurred in, 4; Christ took upon himself the burden of our sins in, 4-5

Glad Tidings Near Cumorah, knowledge of restoration is, 133

Gold Bible Hill, Hill Cumorah has been referred as, 60

Hale, Emma, maiden name of Joseph Smith's wife was, 71; Joseph Smith marries, 71-72

Harris, Martin, a scribe of Joseph Smith was, 83; how Joseph translated the Book of

Peep-stone, description and comments concerning a, 86-87; Hiram Page had a, 87

Peter, John the Baptist acted under direction of , and James and John, 112

Physical attributes of Father and Son, doctrines learned concerning the, 33-34, 40

Pillar of Light, Joseph Smith says he saw a, 24-26

Plates, Joseph Smith sees in vision where, were deposited, 46-47; at Hill Cumorah Joseph Smith sees, in box, 61-62; Joseph Smith obtains, 72-73; a wooden chest made for storing, 73, 77-78; story of men searching for, 85; Joseph Smith delivered to Moroni the, 88; three witnesses saw the, 99-100; description and weight of, 101; two accounts of Mrs. Whitmer seeing the, 130

Preparatory Years, Joseph Smith experienced, 64

Priesthood, the Aaronic, 111; the Melchizedek, 115; explanation concerning the Melchizedek, 109-119

Prince of darkness, at Hill Cumorah Joseph Smith saw, who is Satan, 62

Prophet Joseph Smith, See Smith, Joseph Jr.

Ramah, Jaredite people called the Hill Cumorah, 56-57; last great battle of Jaredite people at, 57-58

Raphael, another name for Enoch is speculated to be, 118; Joseph Smith was visited by, 118

Ripliancum, during time of Jaredites the name of many waters is, 56-58

Rockwell, Orrin Porter, President Brigham Young related a marvelous experience of, 127-128

Sacred Garden, Garden of Eden is a, 1-3; Garden of Gethsemane is a, 3-5; Sacred Grove is a, 5-10

Sacred Grove, located a few hundred yards from the Smith home was the, 8; age of trees of, 8; part of a 15-acre forest included the, 8; twelve to fifteen hundred maple trees were in the, 8; Father and Son appeared in, 8; leaders of Church visited, 8; Mr. Chapman owned farm and, 9; no tree cut from, 9; Church purchased farm and, from Mr. Chapman 9-10; Elder Thomas McKay said, was a garden, 10

Satan, in Sacred Grove, walked and seized Joseph Smith, 22; Joseph learned that, had no power in presence of Father and Son, 40; at Hill Cumorah Joseph Smith sees prince of darkness who is, 62

America described by, 64-65; experiences of, at Hill Cumorah, 53-72; Moroni chastises, 68-69; description of, 42-43; accused of being a money digger was, 71; Emma Hale marries, 71-72; time for obtaining plates and breastplate and Urim and Thummim by, 72; Lucy Smith shown a key or Urim and Thummim by, 73; Lucy Smith tells of struggle carrying plates home by, 73-74; Lucy Smith shown breastplate by, 76-77; how Book of Mormon was translated by, 81-84; Moroni received plates and breastplate and Urim and Thummim from, 88; Seer Stone of, 85-92; three witnesses of Book of Mormon learned by, 96; calling of three witnesses by, 97-98; three witnesses to see sacred items as told by, 97-98; three witnesses saw sacred items with, 100-101; joy of three witnesses and, 105-106; John the Baptist appeared to, and Oliver Cowdery, 111-112; John the Baptist conferred the Aaronic Priesthood to, and Oliver Cowdery, 112; Oliver Cowdery was baptized by, 113; Oliver Cowdery baptized, 113; Oliver Cowdery was ordained the Aaronic Priesthood by, 114; Oliver Cowdery ordained the Aaronic Priesthood to, 114;

Melchizedek Priesthood conferred by Peter and James and John to, and Oliver Cowdery, 1115-116; ancient apostles and prophets visited, 117-119; Twelve Apostles received keys from, 119-122; twice Oliver Cowdery entered the Hill Cumorah with, 123-126; experience of Zelph related by, 131; testimonies of, 132

Smith, Joseph Smith Sr., a decision to move from Vermont to western New York made by, family, 5, Joseph Smith Jr. told by his father, to rest at home, 49; Joseph Smith Jr. commanded by Moroni to speak his father, 51; Joseph Smith Jr. told of Moroni's visit and instructions to his father, 51; Joseph Smith Jr. told to follow Moroni's instruction by his father, 51; head of Smith family was, 54; Joseph Smith was asked who chastised him by, 68-69; Emma was sent by, to tell her husband of men searching for plates, 73; Joseph Smith requested, and Lucy Smith to come to Whitmer home, 98; joy of Joseph Smith and three witnesses expressed to, 105-106

Smith, Lucy Mack, after First Vision Joseph Smith spoke first to his mother, 31; History

experience of, 130-131; two accounts of the plates shown to, 130

Witnesses, law of, 96; Oliver Cowdery and Martin Harris and Peter Whitmer desired and were called to be three, 97; sacred items were to be seen by three, 97-98; sacred items were seen by three, 99-100; the joy of Joseph Smith and, 105-106; testimonies never denied by the three, 107; testimony in Book of Mormon by three, 106-108; testimony in Book of Mormon by eight, 108

Woods, see Sacred Grove

Zelph, Joseph Smith tells of white Lamanite named, 131-132

Zion's Camp, Joseph Smith led volunteers to redeem Zion called, 119

About the Author

Bruce E. Dana is an avid student of the gospel, who served as a missionary in the Northwestern States and Pacific Northwest missions for the Church. He attended Weber State College and Utah State University. For several years, he was a mortgage banker. He has also worked for both the county and federal government and is presently employed as a coordinator.

Brother Dana has served in a wide variety of Church callings and enjoys teaching the doctrines of the gospel. He is married to Brenda Lamb and is the father of eight children.

0 26575 77239 5